WHY GOVERNMENT CAN'T SAVE YOU

WHY GOVERNMENT CAN'T SAVE YOU

DR. JOHN F. MACARTHUR, JR.

WORD PUBLISHING

NASHVILLE

A Thomas Nelson Company

WHY GOVERNMENT CAN'T SAVE YOU
Dr. John F. MacArthur, Jr.

Published by Word Publishing, a unit of Thomas Nelson, Inc.,
P. O. Box 141000, Nashville, Tennessee 37214. All rights reserved.
No portion of this book may be reproduced, stored in a retrieval system,
or transmitted in any form or by any means—electronic, mechanical,
photocopy, recording, or any other—except for brief quotations
in printed reviews, without the prior permission of the publisher.

Unless otherwise indicated, Scripture quotations used in this book are
from the *New King James Version,* copyright © 1979, 1980, 1982
by Thomas Nelson, Inc. Used by permission.

Scripture references identified as KJV are from
the *King James Version* of the Bible.

Scripture references identified as NASB are from
the *New American Standard Bible,* copyright © 1960, 1962, 1963, 1971,
1973, 1975, and 1977 by the Lockman Foundation.
Used by permission.

Scripture references identified NIV are from
the *New International Version,* copyright © 1978
by the New York International Bible Society.
Used by permission of Zondervan Bible Publishers.

Scripture references identified TLB are from *The Living Bible,*
copyright © 1971 by Tyndale House Publishers, Wheaton, Ill.
Used by permission.

Library of Congress Cataloging-in-Publication Data

MacArthur, John, 1939–
  Why government can't save you: an alternative to political activism / by
John F. MacArthur
    p. cm.—(Bible for life series ; 7)
  ISBN 0-8499-5555-6
              1. Christianity and Politics. I. Title.

BR115.P7 M315 2000
261.7—dc21   00-043526   CIP

Printed in the United States of America
00 01 02 03 04 05 PHX 6 5 4 3 2 1

Contents

Introduction

Some years ago a friend asked me a surprising question. He wondered if I'd like to be president of the United States some day.

My answer was a resounding *No!* I would never want to be president because the power to bring righteousness to this country does not now and will never reside in public office. The truth is, I try my best to avoid talking about partisan politics. It's not that I don't have opinions—I have very strong opinions. I avoid it simply because the political arena and its rhetoric have no power to bring about the spiritual transformation our society needs.

Please don't misunderstand me—I don't believe we should remove ourselves from the political process. As Christian citizens, we exercise important responsibilities. Many of the issues at stake today are close to our hearts. The virtues, morals, and principles Christians consider righteous are continually under attack.

While I'm disturbed by the anti-Christian, morally debauched culture we live in and long to see our nation turn to the biblical standard, I'm also concerned about the hostile response to that culture by some believers, churches, and Christian ministries.

Appalled by the lack of biblical morality or sense of justice, believers have been told to take the spiritual battle to the streets. Christians are being urged by their leaders to fight for cultural change by demonstrating, protesting, boycotting, and blockading anything that conflicts with our "traditional values."

I'm concerned about the prevailing mindset that makes political and social activism the primary business of Christianity and reduces faith in Christ to just another political force. Here are a few ways I believe this current trend has inflicted serious harm on the cause of Christ and crippled the effectiveness of evangelism.

First, by looking to human means to reform society and establish Christian values, we've denigrated God's sovereignty over human history and events. Imagine what the world must think of our God. Do we think Him so weak and incapable of caring for us that we prefer using protests and political pressure rather than the spiritual resources He offers? And do we believe He has lost control and we have to get it back for Him?

Second, seeking to bring biblical values to our culture by changing it through fleshly means is a selfish pursuit. The truth is, God never intended for us to be at ease with our culture. What effect will our being comfortable in our culture have on the eternal destination of the men and women in our communities who don't know Christ? Rather than demanding our rights and creating for ourselves a world where we feel safe and accepted, we need to see the deep spiritual needs of the world and concern ourselves with offering people hope through Jesus Christ. That's what being a living sacrifice is all about.

Third, by trying to establish Christian values through earthly methods, we risk creating a false sense of morality. Forcing people to adopt our biblical standards of morality only brings superficial change and hides the real issue—sin and their need for rebirth in Jesus Christ. When people of this world face God's judgment, their "traditional Christian values" won't matter at all—only how they responded to Jesus Christ. That's why pursuing outward change at the expense of inward transformation is both a nearsighted and deadly choice.

Finally, by making activism our priority, we fashion a reputation as rabble-rousing malcontents and foster hostility toward unbelievers that alienates us from them, and them from us. We need to let go of the notion that culture and government are the enemy. It's simply wrong to blame our country's moral disintegration on political parties, liberal conspiracies, or biased media. They have never been the root of the problem. They are the mission field, not the enemy.

Yes, the world is sinful, but must we act surprised or shocked by its sinfulness? How else could sinners act? They are blinded by the powers of darkness and have no spiritual discernment. That's why it's foolish to expect human institutions to produce the kind of righteousness and justice that only God can effect. We can't look to government to uphold or enforce our biblical standards for living. We must do it through consistent, holy living and through the bold proclamation of His Word by the truly redeemed church. When we make that our focus, we'll stop treating the unconverted as our enemy and begin seeing them compassionately as our mission field. Indeed, we are in a battle, but it is a clash of spiritual kingdoms, a battle in which we must use the spiritual weapon of divine truth.

That was certainly our Lord's priority. As He was brought before Pontius Pilate, the Roman governor asked Him, "'Are You the King of the Jews?' . . . Jesus answered, 'My kingdom is not of this world. If My kingdom were of this world, My servants would fight, so that I should not be delivered to the Jews; but now My kingdom is not from here.' Pilate therefore said to Him, 'Are You a king then?' Jesus answered, 'You say rightly that I am a king. For this cause I was born, and for this cause I have come into the world, that I should bear witness to the truth'" (John 18:33, 36-37).

Living the Christian life in an ungodly society is never easy. You'll recall that the message of the Old Testament prophets always cut across the grain of ancient culture. People true to God's Word will do the same today, not because of their political convictions but because of their spiritual convictions.

However, you may still be asking some important, practical questions. What does God say is our responsibility to government? What are Christians to do when the government allows the wholesale slaughter of babies, exalts homosexuality, and denigrates any and every kind of moral standard? Is not taking to the streets in protest a better option than passively letting each trend run its course?

Those are tough but very important questions to ask, and that's my reason for writing this book. I have titled it, *Why Government Can't Save You* for the very reasons I just outlined for you. Only God, through Jesus Christ, can bring about real transformation. In the first chapter, we'll look at the issues more closely and examine in depth what the Bible teaches about political involvement.

Beginning with chapter two, we'll take a survey of sorts about what the apostle Paul in Romans 13 says about the Christian's responsibility to government. That will extend to a look in chapter three at why governments exist.

Paul even goes so far as to include the definitive treatment on the believer's tax-paying responsibility. We'll take a look at that in chapter four. But Paul wasn't the only one to teach on taxes—even Jesus instructed Peter regarding the reasons we must support the government in that way. I think you'll discover some important principles in chapter five.

In chapter six, we'll rejoin our look at Romans 13, but we'll also examine from 1 Peter 2 some of the apostle Peter's teaching on the matter of supporting our governmental leaders.

Just so you don't think that the Bible offers only instruction in this matter, in chapters seven and eight we'll look at the lives of two giants in Scripture—Daniel and Paul—to see how they practiced these principles.

In the last chapter we'll get back to *you*—what ought to be your focus as you live in the midst of an ungodly society. The principles that Paul gave Titus, if followed, will revolutionize your ministry to both believers and unbelievers alike.

And as a reminder of where your allegiance should be, I have included a sermon from Charles Spurgeon on our citizenship in heaven. Only as we continually stay focused on our ultimate destination will we be motivated to spread the good news of salvation in Christ to those who so desperately need Him.

When you finish this book, I think you'll know how to influence your community for the cause of Christ. I believe America's heart can be turned toward God, but only through the power of the Spirit, one person at a time. And you and I have at our disposal the only means to bring genuine, lasting change: God's good news of salvation. So use it for the glory of God's kingdom.

Chapter 1

Political Involvement: A Christian Perspective

Over the past several centuries, people have mistakenly linked democracy and political freedom to Christianity.

Chapter 1

═➤◄(◉)►◄═

Political Involvement: A Christian Perspective

There was a time when nearly everyone could name off all the Ten Commandments, but today most don't even know what the Ten Commandments are. There was also a time when retail stores, dining and entertainment establishments, and all nonessential enterprises would be closed on Sundays out of respect for the Lord's Day. But now for most people in the West it's fairly much business as usual on Sundays. Furthermore, there was a time (not so many years ago), when respectable citizens uniformly disapproved of homosexuality, adultery, and divorce; believed sexual promiscuity was absolutely wrong; disdained cursing or obscene language; saw abortion as unthinkable; and automatically held public officials to high moral and ethical standards. But today many citizens, when polled on such

3

issues, view them either as acceptable practices, civil rights, or inconsequential matters.

How times and the culture have changed! All those past scenarios seem to most unbelievers better suited to the realm of an old novel or book of legends and fables. The strong Christian influence and scriptural standards that shaped Western culture and American society through the end of the nineteenth century have definitely given way to practical atheism and moral relativism. The few vestiges of Christianity in the culture are at best weak and compromising, and to an increasingly pagan society they are cultic and bizarre.

In the United States, political leaders, legislative bodies, and courts during the past half century have adopted, mainly through laws and judicial rulings, a distinctly anti-Christian attitude and agenda. The country has swept away the principles of the Christian worldview under the guises of strict separation of church and state, equal rights, "political correctness," and tolerance.

Evangelical Christians are understandably alarmed and even resentful at what has occurred in contemporary America:

- Public institutions and officials now sanction "alternate lifestyles" (homosexuality) and same-sex unions.
- "Reproductive freedom" (a woman's right to have an abortion) is an accepted viewpoint that's supported by the Supreme Court.
- Schools and government agencies promote "safe sex" for young people (secular sex education that ignores the moral and spiritual issues of premarital sex and

worries only about venereal diseases and unwanted babies).

- "Judicial fairness" gets prime consideration in the court system (criminals exonerated as "victims of their environments," at the disregard of the real victims).
- "True freedom of expression" (pornographic literature, film, and art exhibitions) is all that matters in the arts.

To make matters worse, believers often feel intensified hostilities toward the government when they realize that their tax dollars are funding such ungodly ideas and practices.

During the past twenty-five years, well-meaning Christians have founded a number of evangelical activist organizations and put millions of dollars into them in an ill-conceived effort to counteract the secular undermining of American culture. They have used these groups, along with existing Christian publishing houses and broadcast networks, to lobby hard for a "Christian" political viewpoint and fight back against the prevailing anti-Christian culture. Sadly, those believers have often displayed mean-spirited attitudes and utilized the same kinds of worldly tactics as their unbelieving opponents. The problem with this overall approach should be obvious—believers become antagonistic toward the very lost people God has called them to love and reach with the gospel.

LESSONS FROM HISTORY

There is no denying the historical precedent for political, cultural, and even military activism by professing Christians. But such precedent doesn't make that sort of Christian preoccupation right or biblical. The Crusades during the Middle Ages were waged for the purpose of regaining Christian control of the Holy Lands, yet few believers today would praise that effort. Religious wars and campaigns tinged with political motivation, such as what occurred during the Reformation era in Europe and England are viewed with disapproval, or at best curiosity, by people today. For example, who today can identify with the motivations of France, Spain, Sweden, Denmark, Austria, and some of the German states in the early 1600s to wage a long conflict (Thirty Years' War) whose cause was rooted in the bitter rivalry between Roman Catholic and Protestant rulers as much as it was in nationalistic hostilities? Or how many present-day believers would even partially approve of the Puritans' bloody overthrow, under the leadership of Oliver Cromwell, of the English monarchy in the 1660s and the imposition of their austere view of church, state, and morality on the nation? (The Puritans were particularly cruel to Irish Catholics.)

Over the past several centuries, people have mistakenly linked democracy and political freedom to Christianity. That's why many contemporary evangelicals believe the American Revolution was completely justified, both politically and scripturally. They follow the argumentation of the Declaration of Independence, which declares that life, liberty, and the pursuit of happiness are divinely endowed rights. Therefore those believers say such rights are part of a Christian worldview, worth attaining and defending at all costs, including military insurrection at times. But such a position is contrary to the clear teachings and commands of Romans 13:1–7. So the United States was actually born out of a violation of New Testament principles, and any blessings that God has bestowed on America have come in spite of that disobedience by the Founding Fathers.

Also, many present-day Christian activists seem to be unaware of how much their methodology parallels that of liberal Christians at the turn of the twentieth century. Like those misguided idealists, contemporary evangelicals became enamored of temporal issues at the expense of eternal values. Evangelical activists, in essence, are simply preaching a politically conservative version of the old social gospel, emphasizing social and cultural concerns above spiritual ones. In that framework the government becomes more and more the earthly ally (if he can persuade it to support his special agenda) or enemy (if it stays opposed or unresponsive to his agenda) of the Christian. But the ideal human government can ultimately do nothing to advance God's kingdom, and the worst, most despotic worldly government in the end cannot halt the power of the Holy Spirit or the spread of God's Word.

To gain a thoroughly biblical and Christian perspective on political involvement, we should take to heart the words of the British theologian Robert L. Ottley, delivered at Oxford University more than one hundred years ago:

> The Old Testament may be studied . . . as an instructor in social righteousness. It exhibits the moral government of God as attested in his dealings with nations rather than with individuals; and it was their consciousness of the action and presence of God in history that made the prophets preachers, not merely to their countrymen, but to the world at large. . . . There is indeed significance in the fact that in spite of their ardent zeal for social reform they did not as a rule take

part in political life or demand political reforms. They desired . . . not better institutions but better men.[1]

LESSONS FROM SCRIPTURE

My point is not that Christians should remain totally un-involved in politics or civic activities and causes. They ought to express their political beliefs in the voting booth, and it is all right occasionally to support legitimate measures designed to correct a glaring social or political wrong. Complete non-involvement would be contrary to what God's Word says about doing good in society: "Therefore, as we have opportu-nity, let us do good to all, especially to those who are of the household of faith" (Galatians 6:10; see Titus 3:1–2). It would also display a lack of gratitude for whatever amount of religious freedom the government allows us to enjoy. Furthermore, such pious apathy toward government and politics would reveal a lack of appreciation for the many appropriate legal remedies believers in democracies have for maintaining or improving the civil order. A certain amount of healthy and balanced concern with current trends in government and the commu-nity is acceptable, as long as we realize that such interest is not vital to our spiritual growth, our righteous testimony, or the advancement of the kingdom of Christ. Above all, the believer's political involvement should never displace the pri-ority of preaching and teaching the gospel.

Believers are certainly not prohibited from being directly involved in government as civil servants, as some notable examples in the Old and New Testaments illustrate. Joseph in

Egypt and Daniel in Babylon are two excellent models of servants God used in top governmental positions to further His kingdom. The centurion's servant (Matthew 8:5–13), Zacchaeus the tax collector (Luke 19:1–10), and Cornelius the centurion (Acts 10) all continued in public service even after they experienced the healing or saving power of Christ. (Acts 13:4–12 records that the Roman proconsul Sergius Paulus also remained in office after he was converted.)

The issue again is one of priority. The greatest temporal good we can accomplish through political involvement cannot compare to what the Lord can accomplish through us in the eternal work of His kingdom. Just as God called ancient Israel (Exodus 19:6), He has called the church to be a kingdom of priests, not a kingdom of political activists. The apostle Peter instructs us, "But you are a chosen generation, a royal priesthood, a holy nation, His own special people, that you may proclaim the praises of Him who called you out of darkness into His marvelous light" (1 Peter 2:9).

Political and Social Difficulties

Jesus, as we would expect, perfectly maintained His Father's perspective on these matters, even though He lived in a society that was every bit as pagan and corrupt as today's culture. In many ways it was much worse than any of us in Western nations has ever faced. Cruel tyrants and dictators ruled throughout the region, the institution of slavery was firmly entrenched—everything was the antithesis of democracy. King Herod, the Idumean vassal of Rome who ruled Samaria and Judea, epitomized the godless kind of autocratic rule: "Then Herod, when he saw that he was deceived by the wise men [concerning the whereabouts of the baby Jesus], was exceedingly angry; and he sent forth and put to death all the male children who were in Bethlehem and in all its districts, from two years old and under" (Matthew 2:16).

Furthermore, few of us have experienced the sort of economic and legal oppression that the Romans applied to the Jews of Jesus' day. Tax rates were exorbitant and additional government-sanctioned abuses by the tax collectors exacerbated the financial burden on the people. The Jews in Palestine were afforded almost no civil rights and were treated as an underprivileged minority that could not make an appeal against legal injustices. As a result, some Jews were in constant outward rebellion against Rome.

Fanatical nationalists, known as Zealots, ignored their tax obligations and violently opposed the government. They believed that even recognizing a Gentile ruler was wrong (see Deuteronomy 17:15, "You may not set a foreigner over you, who is not your brother"). Many Zealots became assassins, performing acts of terrorism and violence against both the Romans and other Jews whom they viewed as traitors.

It is also true that the Roman social system was built on slavery. The reality of serious abuses of slaves is part of the historical record. Yet neither Jesus nor any of the apostles attempted to abolish slavery. Instead, they told slaves to be obedient and used slavery as a metaphor for believers who were to submit to their Lord and Master.

Jesus' earthly ministry took place right in the midst of that difficult social and political atmosphere. Many of His followers, including the Twelve, to varying degrees expected Him to free them from Rome's oppressive rule. But our Lord did not come as a political deliverer or social reformer. He never issued a call for such changes, even by peaceful means. Unlike many late twentieth-century evangelicals, Jesus did not rally supporters to some grandiose attempt to "capture the culture" for biblical morality or greater political and religious freedoms. Instead, He did not hesitate to make such clear declarations as, "Render therefore to Caesar the things that are Caesar's, and to God the things that are God's" (Matthew 22:21), and, "The scribes and the Pharisees sit in Moses' seat. Therefore whatever they tell you to observe, that observe and do, but do not do according to their works; for they say, and do not do" (Matthew 23:2–3). The pagan Roman officials and wicked Jewish leaders were not to be emulated, but they were to be obeyed.

Christ, however, was not devoid of care and concern for the daily pain and hardships people endured in their personal lives. The Gospels record His great empathy and compassion for sinners. He applied those attitudes in a tangible, practical way by healing thousands of people of every kind of disease and affliction, often at great personal sacrifice to Himself.

Still, as beneficial and appreciated as His ministry to others' physical needs was, it was not Jesus' first priority. His divine calling was to speak to the hearts and souls of individual men and women. He proclaimed the good news of redemption that could reconcile them to the Father and grant them eternal life. That message far surpasses any agenda for political, social, or economic reform that can preoccupy us. Christ did not come to promote some new social agenda or establish a new moral order. He did come to establish a new spiritual order, the body of believers from throughout the ages that constitutes His church. He did not come to earth to make the old creation moral through social and governmental reform but to make new creatures (His people) holy through the saving power of the gospel and the transforming work of the Holy Spirit.

And our Lord and Savior has commanded us to continue His ministry, with His supreme priorities in view, with the goal that we might advance His kingdom: "All authority has been given to Me in heaven and on earth. Go therefore and make disciples of all the nations, baptizing them in the name of the Father and of the Son and of the Holy Spirit, teaching them to observe all things that I have commanded you; and lo, I am with you always, even to the end of the age" (Matthew 28:18–20).

In the truest sense, the moral, social, and political state of a people is irrelevant to the advance of the gospel. Jesus said that His kingdom was not of this world (John 18:36).

THE REAL BATTLE

We can't protect or expand the cause of Christ by human political and social activism, no matter how great or sincere the efforts. Ours is a spiritual battle against worldly ideologies and dogmas that are arrayed against God, and we achieve victory over them only with the weapon of Scripture. The apostle Paul writes: "For though we walk in the flesh, we do not war according to the flesh. For the weapons of our warfare are not carnal but mighty in God for pulling down strongholds, casting down arguments and every high thing that exalts itself against the knowledge of God, bringing every thought into captivity to the obedience of Christ" (2 Corinthians 10:3–5).

As Paul's words declare, we must reject all that is ungodly and false and never compromise God's standards of righteousness. We can do that partly by desiring the improvement of society's moral standards and partly by approving of measures that would conform government more toward righteousness. We do grieve over the rampant indecency, vulgarity, unchastity, lack of courtesy and respect for others, deceitfulness, self-indulgent materialism, and violence that is corroding society. But in all of our efforts to support what is good and wholesome, reject what is evil and corrupt, and make a profoundly positive impact on our culture, we must use God's methods and maintain scriptural priorities.

God simply is not calling us to wage a culture war that would seek to transform our countries into "Christian nations." To devote all, or even most, of our time, energy, money, and strategy to putting a façade of morality on the world or the appearance of "rightness" over our governmental and political institutions is to badly misunderstand our roles as Christians in a spiritually lost world.

God has above all else called the church to bring sinful people to salvation through Jesus Christ. Even as the apostle Paul described his mission to unbelievers, so it is the primary task of all Christians to reach out to the lost "to open their eyes, in order to turn them from darkness to light and from the power of Satan to God, that they may receive forgiveness of sins and an inheritance among those who are sanctified by faith in [Christ]" (Acts 26:18; see also Exodus 19:6; 1 Peter 2:5, 9). If we do not evangelize the lost and make disciples of new converts, nothing else we do for people—no matter how beneficial it seems—is of any eternal consequence. Whether a person is an atheist or a theist, a criminal or a model citizen, sexually promiscuous and perverse or strictly moral and virtuous, a greedy materialist or a gracious philanthropist—if he does not have a saving relationship with Christ, he is going to hell. It makes no difference if an unsaved person is strongly proabortion or antiabortion, a political liberal or a conservative, a prostitute or a police officer, he will spend eternity apart from God unless he repents and believes the gospel.

When the church takes a stance that emphasizes political activism and social moralizing, it always diverts energy and resources away from evangelization. Such an antagonistic position toward the established secular culture invariably leads believers to feel hostile not only to unsaved government leaders with whom they disagree, but also antagonistic toward the unsaved residents of that culture—neighbors and fellow citizens they ought to love, pray for, and share the gospel with. To me it is unthinkable that we become enemies of the very people we seek to win to Christ, our potential brothers and sisters in the Lord.

Author John Seel pens words that apply in principle to Christians everywhere and summarize well the believer's perspective on political involvement:

> A politicized faith not only blurs our priorities, but weakens our loyalties. Our primary citizenship is not on earth but in heaven. . . . Though few evangelicals would deny this truth in theory, the language of our spiritual citizenship frequently gets wrapped in the red, white and blue. Rather than acting as resident aliens of a heavenly kingdom, too often we sound [and act] like resident apologists for a Christian America. . . . Unless we reject the false reliance on the illusion of Christian America, evangelicalism will continue to distort the gospel and thwart a genuine biblical identity.
>
> American evangelicalism is now covered by layers

and layers of historically shaped attitudes that obscure our original biblical core.[2]

By means of faithful preaching and godly living, believers are to be the conscience of whatever nation they reside in. They are to confront the culture not with the political and social activism of man's wisdom—whether it be someone else's or their own—but with the spiritual power of God's Word. Using temporal methods to promote legislative and judicial change, and resorting to external efforts of lobbying and intimidation to achieve some sort of "Christian morality" in society is not our calling—and has no eternal value. Only the gospel rescues sinners from sin, death, and hell.

Chapter 2

---·◉·---

Our Responsibility to Authority

God commands that we be model citizens,
ones who are law-abiding, obedient, and respectful
toward governmental authority.

Chapter 2

Our Responsibility to Authority

We live in an era that questions authority. It has been that way for more than forty years. First the tumultuous years of the sixties and seventies witnessed civil disobedience (sometimes violent) that accompanied the civil rights movement and the anti-Vietnam war protests. During those years, people in the United States were also shocked by three major assassinations (President John F. Kennedy; civil rights leader Dr. Martin Luther King, Jr.; Senator Robert F. Kennedy). Following those events, the average person became more and more accustomed to hearing about challenges against the governmental status quo, such as the dissolution of the former Soviet Union, the end of the apartheid system in South Africa, and the popular but unsuccessful democracy movement in China.

In the cases of the Soviet Union and South Africa, it has become clear that, no matter how harsh the exercise of power was in the past, the newfound "freedom" resulting from the fall of those established governments has created chaos and crime at levels never known under the former regimes. Such changes have made life for most people in those countries more difficult and less safe.

Add to all those the various more gradual and long-term challenges to authority during the past three decades, like the feminist movement, the relentless push for homosexual rights, environmental activism, the rise of antigovernment and antitax "state militia" groups, and assorted coalitions for economic and political reform, and the average person is left with his mind spinning. He or she quite understandably wonders, What is the total significance of such phenomena and how, if at all, should such attempts to influence or over-turn authority affect my attitudes and actions?

For believers, the answer is simple and straightforward: "Let every soul be subject to the governing authorities" (Romans 13:1). In the widest sense, this command applies to all people, but the apostle Paul was writing specifically to Christians and declaring, in essence, that Christianity and good citizenship go hand in hand. Paul's admonition goes far beyond the mere obedience of various civil laws. His concept of good citizenship, inspired by the Holy Spirit, also encompasses a sincere honor and respect for all official authority. Such an attitude is vital regarding government because government officials are God's agents for maintaining order and justice in society.

THE PRINCIPLE OF CIVIL OBEDIENCE

God commands that we be model citizens, ones who are law-abiding, obedient, and respectful toward governmental authority. When observing our relationship to those over us, people should never characterize us as rabble-rousers, rebels, or insolent critics. As we suggested in chapter one, the Lord expects us to speak out against sin, injustice, immorality, and ungodliness with courage and diligence. But we must do so in a law-abiding manner, according to the civil laws that legislative bodies and governing officials have established for us. The church is to be a godly society within the larger ungodly society, living peaceably and exhibiting good works through the transformed lives of its members. Only in those ways will we truly affect society and allow the Holy Spirit to draw unconverted people to the saving power of God.

"Be subject to" in Romans 13:1 is from the familiar Greek New Testament term *hupotasso,* which was primarily a military word that denoted soldiers ranked under and subject to the absolute authority of a superior officer. Paul used the expression in the passive imperative, which makes it a command and indicates that believers should willingly place themselves under all government leaders, no matter who those officials are.

Notice that the apostle, under the inspiration of the Holy Spirit, gives this command without qualification or condition. We are to obey *every* civil authority, no matter how immoral, cruel, ungodly, or incompetent he or she might be. *Any* government is better than anarchy, but those character qualities and leadership traits in rulers can make obedience difficult.

21

But in another letter Paul exhorts us "that supplications, prayers, intercessions, and giving of thanks be made for all men, for kings and all who are in authority, that we may lead a quiet and peaceable life in all godliness and reverence" (1 Timothy 2:1–2; see 1 Thessalonians 4:11–12; Titus 3:1–2).

Civil obedience was also an Old Testament principle. Even while the Jews were held as captives in the pagan country of Babylon, God through the prophet Jeremiah commanded them, "Seek the peace of the city where I have caused you to be carried away captive, and pray to the LORD for it; for in its peace you will have peace" (Jeremiah 29:7).

But the inspired writers, early in Old Testament history, recognized there is one exception or limitation to our divinely mandated obligation of civil obedience: whenever an ordinance or official command would require that we disobey God's will or His Word.

The pharaoh in Egypt once ordered the killing of all Israelite male babies by their Jewish midwives. But the two midwives involved, Shiphrah and Puah, knew that murder was wrong and refused to comply with the monarch's decree. "The midwives feared God, and did not do as the king of Egypt commanded them, but saved the male children alive" (Exodus 1:17). Because the two women were faithful to the Lord's teaching, He affirmed their civil disobedience and "dealt well with the midwives, and the people multiplied and grew very mighty" (verse 20).

Righteous Civil Disobedience in Daniel

The Book of Daniel records three significant accounts of justifiable civil disobedience. First, when Daniel and his three

Jewish countrymen, as exiles in a foreign land, were ordered by the king of Babylon to eat "a daily provision of the king's delicacies and of the wine which he drank" (Daniel 1:5), they politely declined to do so. Otherwise they would have had to defile themselves by breaking the Mosaic dietary laws. Here is the gracious alternative Daniel proposed to one of the king's officials: "'Please test your servants for ten days, and let them give us vegetables to eat and water to drink. Then let our appearance be examined before you, and the appearance of the young men who eat the portion of the king's delicacies; and as you see fit, so deal with your servants.' So he consented with them in this matter, and tested them ten days" (Daniel 1:12–14). God was pleased to allow them to pass the test, "and at the end of ten days their features appeared better and fatter in flesh than all the young men who ate the portion of the king's delicacies" (verse 15).

Even while declining to do something God's law wouldn't allow, Daniel and his friends, as godly men, respected the human authority they were under. As spokesman for the group, Daniel did not demand the right to their beliefs, but deferentially "requested of the chief of the eunuchs that he might not defile himself" (verse 8) and even called himself and his friends the king's "servants." Those four faithful men could still obey God without self-righteously disrespecting, contending with, or putting down the civil authority.

A second account of legitimate civil disobedience in the Book of Daniel concerns how Daniel's three colleagues (Shadrach, Meshach, and Abed-Nego) refused to engage in the open idolatry that King Nebuchadnezzar's command would have required. When the king ordered the three men and all his subjects to worship his gods and the special golden image he had erected, the three told him, "We have no need to answer you in this matter. If that is the case, our God whom we serve is able to deliver us from the burning fiery furnace, and He will deliver us from your hand, O king. But if not, let it be known to you, O king, that we do not serve your gods, nor will we worship the gold image which you have set up" (Daniel 3:16–18). The Lord again honored their faithfulness and spared them from the fatal consequences of Nebuchadnezzar's fiery furnace (verses 24–27).

The third example of righteous civil disobedience in Daniel is the well-known report of Daniel in the lions' den. He submitted himself to possible death at the jaws of the lions rather than obey King Darius's decree that sought to keep him from worshiping the true God (Daniel 6:7–23). God again honored the wisdom and discernment of a servant who faithfully adhered to His truth rather than a royal edict, and did so with dignity and respect (verses 21, 23).

The New Testament also contains a noteworthy, memorable example of the proper exception to civil obedience. In the earliest days of the church, the religious leaders tried to prohibit Peter and John from proclaiming Jesus' teachings, but the apostles told them, "Whether it is right in the sight of God to listen to you more than to God, you judge. For we cannot but speak the things which we have seen and heard" (Acts 4:19–20). Christ had commissioned them to take the gospel to the whole world (Mark 16:15; Matthew 28:19–20); thus for the disciples to obey those human rulers they would have had to disobey their Master—not something Peter and John were willing to do. So the two apostles kept on preaching the gospel and received another warning from the Jewish leaders. However, that still did not deter them. Instead, "Peter and the other apostles answered and said, 'We ought to obey God rather than men'" (Acts 5:29).

Most of us will seldom face the need to "obey God rather than men." Nearly always it will be God's will that we obey, both from His Word and through human authority. Likewise, our churches ought to obey ordinances and regulations concerning zoning, fire safety, structural standards, building permits, and every other law that does not conflict with Scripture. In all such matters we are to obey local, regional, and national government directives willingly, without grumbling or complaining (see Philippians 2:14–16). Even on those rare occasions when we must follow the exception principle regarding civil obedience, we should do so respectfully, prepared to suffer the consequences or penalties that may result. In those instances, we must heed Peter's instruction that "it is better, if it is the will of God, to suffer for doing good than for doing evil" (1 Peter 3:17). And above all we should never, in any of our dealings with authority (or in any societal relationships), "suffer as a murderer, a thief, an evildoer, or as a busybody in other people's matters" (4:15).

A contemporary and applicable example that relates to 1 Peter 4:15 is the extreme protest strategy of some antiabortion groups, some of which claim to be Christian. During the past decade, such groups have disregarded police orders not to block entrances to abortion clinics, bombed some clinics, and shot and killed clinic workers and doctors—all in the name of legitimate civil disobedience. In 1994 a jury convicted a former Presbyterian minister of killing an abortion doctor, and the former minister reacted by confidently predicting he would go straight to heaven if executed for his actions. It is certainly not honorable as a professed believer to be in such a position—it's disgraceful.

It's similarly disgraceful and wrong for believers in any way to condone disruptive or harmful antihomosexual protests. I'm especially dismayed when I hear reports of ardent fundamentalists, such as a pastor and his extended family in Kansas, who brashly and venomously use an Internet page to promote hatred of homosexuals. In the fall of 1998 that man and his supporters reportedly even callously and disrespectfully demonstrated at the funeral of the murdered gay college student from the University of Wyoming.

By making such criticisms of those professed Christians who misunderstand, abuse, or disobey the biblical principles of civil obedience and its legitimate exceptions, I want to affirm clearly that I am still unalterably opposed to the sins of abortion and homosexuality. God's Word plainly teaches the sanctity of life (Exodus 20:13; 21:22–25; Job 10:8–12; Psalm 139:13–16; Matthew 18:6) and the sinfulness of homosexuality (Leviticus 18:22; 20:13; Romans 1:26–27; 1 Corinthians 6:9). My point is that hateful, extremist attitudes and actions, expressed under the guise of Christian social activism and biblical morality, are wrong. Whenever we seek to promote what is right and redress what is wrong, or when we believe legitimate civil disobedience is appropriate, we must ask God for discernment and the grace to use biblical principles. Otherwise, we deserve the apostle Peter's label "busybody" ("troublesome meddler," NASB).

Secular authority may persecute us in various ways because of our Christian convictions. However, there is no type of persecution that should cause us to revolt against the government. It should only cause us to patiently endure the trial and persevere in righteousness. Christ commands us to be aware, concerned, and careful about what is going on in our culture and the world and how it affects us (Matthew 10:16). But that posture must not be our sole preoccupation. Our Lord wants us to live above reproach, free of worry, rancor, or self-righteousness toward worldly authorities.

JUSTIFICATION FOR CIVIL OBEDIENCE

Regardless of the numerous immoral, unjust, and ungodly failures of secular government, believers are to pray and seek to influence the world for Christ by godly, selfless, and peaceful living under that authority, not by protests against the government or by acts of civil disobedience. The apostle Paul in Romans 13 asserts three reasons we should adhere diligently to the principle of civil obedience: (1) human government has been decreed by God, (2) disobeying government means we are disobeying God's institution, and (3) those who rebel against government will be punished.

Satan's Power in Government

Romans 13:1 concludes with this statement, "For there is no authority except from God, and the authorities that exist are appointed by God." In whatever forms it exists, government and its authority derive directly from God and exist to benefit human society. Like marriage, government is a universal institution that is valid regardless of place, circumstance, or other considerations.

No matter what form it takes, all human government that has ever existed (or ever will exist), in any nation, at any level, as a part of any ethnic group, has been under God's sovereign control, because all "power belongs to God" (Psalm 62:11). In fact, the entire universe, including Satan and his demons, is subject to the omnipotent, omniscient will of the Creator. Without exception, the power any leader, political party, or agency wields is delegated and circumscribed by God. Therefore, it only makes sense biblically that we ought to obey the government because its one and only source is God.

Within the context of His total authority, God has permitted Satan great but not unlimited power over the people and affairs of this world. Satan did not directly cause mankind's fall into sin, but his sinister and evil temptation hastened Adam and Eve's disobedience of God, which was the first sin and a characteristic passed on to all their posterity. Ever since that tragic episode in the Garden, the devil has waged a relentless, multifaceted campaign to get men and women to yield to their naturally sinful impulses and defy God.

Consequently, "the whole world lies under the sway of the wicked one" (1 John 5:19), who is "now the ruler of this world" (John 12:31; see also 14:30; 16:11). When Satan tempted Jesus, our Lord did not dispute his claim to "all the kingdoms of the world" or his ability to give Him "all this authority. . .and their glory; for this has been delivered to me [Satan], and I give it to whomever I wish" (Luke 4:5–6).

In both Isaiah 14:12–17 and Ezekiel 28:12–16, Satan is closely identified with the kings of the nations involved (Babylon, Tyre; see Daniel 10:5–14). Thus a clear pattern emerges from Scripture. God instituted government to fulfill

His plan for maintaining civil and social order. However, He has allowed many, if not most, regimes throughout history to be strongly influenced by Satan and become the vehicles for promoting satanic activity.

The evil, ruthless, totalitarian governments of Nazi Germany, Imperial Japan, the Soviet Union, and Communist China illustrate that point, as do the ancient autocratic empires of Egypt, Assyria, Babylon, and Rome. None of those examples, or any of the more contemporary ones (Iraq, Cuba, Libya, North Korea, the former Iron Curtain countries), permits us a waiver on God's command to obey civil authority. In fact, it impresses me that under the restrictive, totalitarian, and atheistic governments of the Soviet Union and China the church has flourished and grown stronger than anywhere in the world. At the same time, the professing church within the free and democratic environments of Western Europe and Japan is small, weak, and dead.

If government was originally decreed by God and is a crucial part of His plan for fallen mankind, then we must, with His help, respect and obey it. The apostle Paul, before the unbelieving philosophers on Athens' Mars Hill, further alluded to this divine principle: "God, who made the world and everything in it, since He is Lord of heaven and earth, does not dwell in temples made with hands. Nor is He worshiped with men's hands, as though He needed anything, since He gives to all life, breath, and all things. And He has made from one blood every nation of men to dwell on all the face of the earth, and has determined their preappointed times and the boundaries of their dwellings" (Acts 17:24–26).

Resisting Government

The second logical reason Christians should hold to the principle of civil obedience is quite simple: "Therefore whoever resists the authority resists the ordinance of God" (Romans 13:2). Clearly, if we rebel against the government God has established for us to be under, we are rebelling against God Himself.

God demonstrated to the Israelites in the Book of Numbers just how seriously He views any sort of rebellion against proper authority. He had chosen Moses to be the lawgiver and leader of Israel, the man He would use to deliver the nation from Egypt, through the wilderness, and into the promised land. At the same time God had named Moses' brother Aaron to be the first high priest. But somewhere along the trek through the wilderness, a significant group of rebels, led by Korah, Dathan, Abiram, and On, "gathered together against Moses and Aaron, and said to them, 'You take too much upon yourselves, for all the congregation is holy, every one of them, and the LORD is among them. Why then do you exalt yourselves above the assembly of the LORD? . . . Is it a small thing that you have brought us up out of a land flowing with milk and honey, to kill us in the wilderness, that you should keep acting like a prince over us?'" (Numbers 16:3, 13).

The group's insolent challenge to Moses' authority was such an affront to God that He soon punished the rebels: "The ground split apart under them, and the earth opened its mouth and swallowed them up, with their households and all the men with Korah, with all their goods. . . . And a fire came out from the LORD and consumed the two hundred and fifty men [rebels] who were offering incense" (verses 31–35). But amazingly that instance of severe judgment was not the end of the story. Instead of reaffirming their submission to God's authority, many of the Israelites revealed an intensified hostility toward His leaders. "On the next day all the congregation of the children of Israel murmured against Moses and Aaron, saying, 'You have killed the people of the LORD'" (verse 41). A further attitude of defiance against His leaders required the Lord to respond by sending a punishing plague that killed "fourteen thousand seven hundred, besides those who died in the Korah incident" (verse 49). Finally Aaron intervened with prayer and the making of atonement for the people, which saved the remaining Israelites from death (verses 46–48).

Before we even consider participating in active opposition to official authority, it's worth remembering commentator Robert Haldane's summary of the significance of civil disobedience: "The people of God then ought to consider resistance to the government under which they live as a very awful crime, even as resistance to God Himself."[1]

Punishment of Resistance

Today we do not see the direct and open judgment of God on sinners who defy civil authority. But there is at least the potential that those who resist government will be punished, if the authorities follow Paul's principle in Romans 13:2 that "those who resist will bring judgment on themselves."

Jesus Himself affirmed this principle at the very time the authorities were arresting Him in Gethsemane, just prior to His unjust but God-ordained death on the cross. Peter drew a sword to fight the soldiers who came to take Jesus captive.

To Peter and the other disciples, that seemed to be a legitimate time to oppose the civil authorities. But Christ commanded Peter, "Put your sword in its place, for all who take the sword will perish by the sword" (Matthew 26:52). Our Lord was saying that no matter how justified you might think it is to take up arms and resist the authorities, even to the extreme of killing for your cause, government still has the right in those situations to execute you as a murderer.

Five biblically based objectives should be a part of any effective punishment.

1. *Fit the offense.* Perhaps the civil authorities in today's "sophisticated" culture could more consistently prevent disrespect and disregard for their authority, and better orchestrate a reduction of the general crime rate, if punishment were meted out according to biblical principles. In the Old Testament, God's leaders viewed punishment as a matter of justice, and they administered it as an appropriate retribution to fit the particular offense: "Life shall be for life, eye for eye, tooth for tooth, hand for hand, foot for foot" (Deuteronomy 19:21). God actually gave this much-maligned precept of "eye for eye" to prevent over-punishment as well as under-punishment. This principle, if implemented as God designed, will be administered by the appropriate government agency and not by victims who are seeking personal revenge.

2. *Viewed as a deterrent to crime.* If this truth is properly understood and applied, guilty persons will be discouraged from committing further offenses and others will not want to follow their unlawful example. "And all the people shall hear and fear, and no longer act presumptuously" (Deuteronomy 17:13; see also 13:11; 19:20).

3. *Administered impartially.* Those who commit crimes will be convicted and punished regardless of how rich or poor they are, how prestigious or obscure their status in the community is, or how influential or noninfluential their friends and relatives are (see Deuteronomy 13:6–9).

4. *Applied without delay.* "Then it shall be, if the wicked man deserves to be beaten, that the judge will cause him to lie down and be beaten in his presence, according to his guilt, with a certain number of blows" (Deuteronomy 25:2). The constitutions of the United States and most other democracies contain provisions for speedy trial and punishment, but sad to say, those standards are seldom observed by judges and the judicial systems. Apparently even in Solomon's day officials disregarded the principle, prompting his warning in Ecclesiastes 8:11, "Because the sentence against an evil work is not executed speedily, therefore the heart of the sons of men is fully set in them to do evil."

5. *Balanced with mercy and rehabilitation.* In Moses' day, here's what the judge could prescribe for the convicted person: "Forty blows he may give him and no more, lest he should exceed this and beat him with many blows above these, and your brother be humiliated in your sight" (Deuteronomy 25:3). Once someone suffers the penalty for wrongdoing, he or she should be accepted back into society and encouraged to be a law-abiding citizen.

Is it any wonder that authority is flouted at every level these days? Not really, when you consider how regularly the preceding biblical principles go unnoticed and unapplied because people, from government officials to average citizens, are ignorant of them. Even when people have some knowledge of the divine role and purpose in government, they tend to disregard, distort, or misapply the biblical standards. But there is a better way.

We carry out our responsibility toward authority and display a God-honoring desire that everyone respect and obey government, being aware of the scriptural consequences for civil disobedience, when we heed the apostle Paul's instructions to Timothy: "Therefore I exhort first of all that supplications, prayers, intercessions, and giving of thanks be made for all men, for kings and all who are in authority, that we may lead a quiet and peaceable life in all godliness and reverence. For this is good and acceptable in the sight of God our Savior, who desires all men to be saved and to come to the knowledge of the truth" (1 Timothy 2:1–4).

Notice that Paul is not at all commanding us to pray for the removal from office of evil rulers or those who are politically "incompatible" with our views. And it is not merely an exhortation for us to pray that our leaders be wise and just, but that they would eventually repent, believe the gospel, and be saved. While the contemporary church seems to have largely forgotten that the priorities for effecting change in society are faithful prayer, godly living, and diligent evangelism rather than persistent lobbying, self-righteous confrontation, and political organizing, the ancient church had its priorities in good order. The church father Tertullian wrote,

> Without ceasing, for all our emperors we offer prayer.
> We pray for life prolonged; for security to the empire;
> for protection to the imperial house; for brave armies,
> a faithful senate, a virtuous people, the world at rest,
> whatever, as man or Caesar, an emperor would wish.
> These things I cannot ask from any but the God from

whom I know I shall obtain them, both because He alone bestows them and because I have claims upon Him for their gift, as being a servant of His, rendering homage to Him alone. . . .

Do you, then, who think that we care nothing for the welfare of Caesar, look into God's revelations, examine our sacred books, which we do not keep in hiding, and which many accidents put into the hands of those who are not of us. Learn from them that a large benevolence is enjoined upon us, even so far as to supplicate God for our enemies, and to beseech blessings on our persecutors. Who, then, are greater enemies and persecutors of Christians, than the very parties with treason against whom we are charged? Nay, even in terms, and most clearly, the Scripture says, "Pray for kings, and rulers, and powers, that all may be peace with you."

We know that a mighty shock impending over the whole earth—in fact, the very end of all things threatening dreadful woes—is only retarded by the continued existence of the Roman empire. We have no desire, then, to be overtaken by these dire events; and in praying that their coming may be delayed, we are lending our aid to Rome's duration.[2]

Thus the ancient church, often during periods of the worst persecution against it, prayed for unbelieving and dictatorial rulers. If we truly desire to fulfill our citizenship responsibilities—which include submission to and respect for the authorities—and thereby positively influence our culture as the early believers did theirs, we must follow their example.

Chapter 3

The Biblical Purpose of Government

You can settle the argument over government's basic purpose and the extent of its activities much more easily if you simply use Scripture as the starting point.

Chapter 3

The Biblical Purpose of Government

Every four years in the United States the great debate returns. It's not always conducted in the most dignified fashion; the most important issues are often distorted or simply ignored. Superficial issues of style and personality usually receive way too much focus, and more and more people grow weary of the entire process. Nevertheless, it draws much attention in the news media. Of course, I'm referring to the national political campaigns in which Americans vote for president, members of Congress, and, perhaps, certain state and local offices.

Those campaigns, largely reduced to mindless sound bites, may not meet all the classic requirements of genuine debate—clear delineation of the major issue, thorough discussion of both sides of the argument, respectful disagreement with the opponent's position (without resorting to personality attacks)—but they generally derive from an underlying philosophical debate over the basic nature of government. The more liberal candidate will usually argue for an expansionist, involved role for government (for example, it should spend more to provide additional social services; it should regulate big business; it should subsidize agriculture), whereas the more conservative candidate will usually argue for a limited role for government (for instance, tax cuts, less bureaucracy and red tape, more focus on national security than social issues).

But the search for government's most appropriate role and purpose has been going on since the founding of the United States, since the contrasting views expressed by Thomas Jefferson and Alexander Hamilton during George Washington's first administration:

> When in February, 1791, Washington called upon Jefferson and Hamilton to submit their opinions on the constitutionality of legislation chartering a Bank of the United States, national political affiliations had already been well defined in terms of broad and basic interests. Though the letters they wrote in reply were couched in the language of the Constitution, the rival Secretaries wrote primarily as leaders of their respective parties. Fearful of extending the powers of an administration so deeply committed to the interests of Federalism, Jefferson spoke the mind of his party when he declared for a "strict" construction of the Constitution: his was a philosophy of limited government. Congress, he argued, had been delegated specifically enumerated powers; its further power "to make all laws necessary and proper" for carrying them into execution must not

be loosely defined. "Necessary and proper," wrote Jefferson, mean "essential." A bank was not essential for carrying out the enumerated powers; therefore the Bank Bill was clearly unconstitutional.

For those whose interests were so well served by the ever more powerful Federalist-dominated central government, Hamilton as vigorously defended the Bank Bill. His was a "loose" or "broad" construction of the Constitution. Implied in the Constitution, wrote the conservative Secretary, was the power to pass even those measures that were "no more than needful, requisite, incidental, useful, or conducive to" carrying out the enumerated powers; the Bank Bill fell into this category and therefore was constitutional. Ultimately Washington accepted Hamilton's opinion and signed the bill. Since that time the doctrine of "implied powers" has been used to extend the functions of government to a point even Hamilton could not have foreseen.[1]

You can settle the argument over government's basic purpose and the extent of its activities much more easily if you simply use Scripture as the starting point. And that brings us back to the apostle Paul's important teaching on the believer and government in Romans 13. As he continues to encourage and exhort us regarding the necessity to obey official authority, Paul identifies three basic purposes for the existence and role of government: (1) it restrains evil, (2) it promotes good, and (3) it is empowered by God to punish wrongdoers and the disobedient.

RESTRAINS EVIL

One of God's ordained roles for government is for it to restrain evil by placing sufficient fear into the hearts of wrongdoers. Romans 13:3 says, "For rulers are not a terror to good works, but to evil."

The word "terror" in the original comes from the same root that gives us the English term *phobia.* The civil authorities should produce that kind of fear in the lives of those who perpetrate evil. Proper government will not be a terror to those citizens who perform good works, that category of deeds which is inherently good. Rather it will be a source of profound terror for those disobedient, lawbreaking citizens who engage in that category of deeds which is inherently evil. Throughout history, even the most wicked of governments have been a deterrent to major crimes such as murder, rape, and theft. Although it hardly justifies totalitarian systems, the reality is that those regimes often experience lower crime rates than do democratic nations. In strict Islamic countries, certain and severe punishment has drastically reduced the rate of violent crimes.

The point is, even ungodly, worldly rulers have a basic awareness of morality. That's because of what happened to Adam and Eve at the beginning of history: "Then the LORD God took the man and put him in the garden of Eden to tend and keep it. And the LORD God commanded the man, saying, 'Of every tree of the garden you may freely eat; but of the tree of the knowledge of good and evil you shall not eat, for in the day that you eat of it you shall surely die'" (Genesis 2:15–17). But the man and his wife did not obey God's command

(Genesis 3:1–7); and when they sinned and ate from the forbidden tree, they acquired a knowledge of good and evil that ever since has been passed on to *all* their descendants (see verse 22; Romans 5:12). Therefore every man and woman who is born has an innate knowledge of right and wrong. That knowledge is the basis of human conscience for both the saved and the unsaved. "When Gentiles, who do not have the law, by nature do the things in the law, these, although not having the law, are a law to themselves, who show the work of the law written in their hearts, their conscience also bearing witness, and between themselves their thoughts accusing or else excusing them" (Romans 2:14–15; see also 1:18–19).

Therefore, because of God's natural revelation (conscience and reason) and His universal common grace, even unconverted government leaders intuitively know good from evil and thus realize that part of their governing responsibility is to punish evil behavior. They understand that basic morality is crucial to a viable social order and that a culture can't flourish with a rampant and unpunished presence of violence, corruption, murder, and sexual immorality.

Even the poorest form of government is better than no government at all. It's frightening to imagine what would occur in any society in which no one was in charge—anarchy is disastrous. If citizens had only themselves to protect their lives and property, strife would result almost immediately and soon any order would collapse. To prevent such a bleak scenario, God established human government to restrain evildoers and lawbreakers.

PROTECTS AND SUPPORTS

The second biblical purpose of civil government is to promote the public good: "Do you want to be unafraid of the authority? Do what is good, and you will have praise from the same. For he is God's minister to you for good" (Romans 13:3–4).

Historically, governments have treated good citizens—those who have been peaceful and supportive of their governments—favorably and fairly. If you are that kind of citizen, you generally will have no reason to be afraid of the authorities. They will oftentimes even be happy to praise you for doing what is right and being a positive influence in the community.

It's entirely appropriate for believers to look to the government at certain times for protection and support. The apostle Paul did that when he used his Roman citizenship to appeal to Caesar for justice (Acts 25:11). Paul also relied on the law's protection during his third missionary journey. In Ephesus, Demetrius the silversmith incited a mob against him, and the town clerk took Paul into protective custody to rescue him from the riotous crowd. The clerk took seriously his responsibility as an advocate of what is good and right when he told the unruly throng, "Therefore, if Demetrius and his fellow craftsmen have a case against anyone, the courts are open and there are proconsuls. Let them bring charges against one another. But if you have any other inquiry to make, it shall be determined in the lawful assembly" (Acts 19:38–39).

By looking out for you and protecting your legitimate rights and interests, any government official is "God's minister" or servant (the Greek word used in Romans 13:4 is *diakonos*, "deacon") on your behalf. Such rulers, whether presidents or prime ministers, senators or members of parliament, high court justices, county commissioners or supervisors, or members of a city council, are due honor and respect as servants of God. Regardless of their personal beliefs about our relationship to God, they represent Him and are doing His work (whether they realize it or not) by promoting peace, justice, and safety among their subjects.

Robert Haldane writes this about government's positive role:

> The institution of civil government is a dispensation of mercy, and its existence is so indispensable, that the moment it ceases under one form, it re-establishes itself in another. The world, ever since the fall, when the dominion of one part of the human race over another was immediately introduced (Gen. 3:16), has been in such a state of corruption and depravity, that without the powerful obstacle presented by civil government to the selfish and malignant passions of men, it would be better to live among the beasts of the forest than in human society. As soon as its restraints are removed, man shows himself in his real character. When there was no king in Israel, and every man did that which was right in his own eyes, we see in the last three chapters of the Book of Judges what were the dreadful consequences.[2]

PUNISHES LAWBREAKERS

Finally, government exists as an institution that God has ordained to punish evil lawbreakers. As a result, those who are not law-abiding citizens and who engage in evil deeds have reason to fear the authorities. Paul states the warning this way: "But if you do evil, be afraid; for he does not bear the sword in vain; for he is God's minister, an avenger to execute wrath on him who practices evil" (Romans 13:4).

Capital Punishment

The sword is a weapon used to maim and kill. Therefore Paul mentions it as a symbol of government's right to punish crimes. That right includes the prerogative to impose the death penalty for those serious crimes that warrant the ultimate punishment. God instituted the death penalty early in humanity's existence. "Whoever sheds man's blood, by man his blood shall be shed; for in the image of God He made man" (Genesis 9:6; see also Matthew 26:52). The lives of men and women are sacred because they were created in God's image. If someone commits murder, that person should have to give up his own life. And officials should administer capital punishment expeditiously, without pity or partiality (see Deuteronomy 13:6–10; 19:13, 20–21; 25:2–3).

When Paul appeared before Festus and appealed his case to Caesar, he recognized the legitimacy of capital punishment and said he was willing to accept it if found guilty of a capital offense. "For if I am an offender, or have committed anything deserving of death, I do not object to dying" (Acts 25:11).

Robert Duncan Culver expounds further on the necessity of government's fulfilling its role as a punisher of lawbreakers:

> What must not be lost sight of is that, unpleasant as is the task of the jailor and the use of the whip, the cell, the noose, the guillotine, these things stand behind the stability of civilized society, and they stand there necessarily, for God has declared it so, in harmony with reality, rather than with apostate sociological opinion. Government, with its coercive powers, is a social necessity, but one determined by the Creator, not by the statistical tables of some university social research staff! No society can successfully vote fines, imprisonment, corporal and capital punishment away permanently. The society which tries has lost touch with realities of man (his fallen sinful state), realities of the world, and the truth of divine revelation in nature, man's conscience, and the Bible.[3]

Whenever a nation rejects capital punishment—as the United States did during the late 1960s and early 1970s, and other Western countries have done to the present day—even for heinous offenses such as murder, God places it under blood guiltiness. Following history's very first murder, "The Lord said to Cain, 'Where is Abel your brother?' He said, 'I do not know. Am I my brother's keeper?' And He said, 'What have you done? The voice of your brother's blood cries out to Me from the ground'" (Genesis 4:9–10). God spared Cain from the death penalty, but as we noted earlier, He did eventually establish capital punishment for murder (Genesis 9:6). Later on, as part of the law He gave Moses, the Lord stated, "So you shall not pollute the land where you are; for blood defiles the land, and no atonement can be made for the land, for the blood that is shed on it, except by the blood of him who shed it" (Numbers 35:33).

Prison

At this point it's not unreasonable to ask, What about the role of prisons? Aren't they serving to punish lawbreakers? Let's take a brief look at what Scripture and redemptive history say about this issue.

First, it is interesting to note that, although pagan nations around Israel commonly utilized prisons in biblical times, there is little record that the ancient Israelites used them. Instead, the Jews either executed criminals promptly or required them to work and pay reparations to their victims. One of the few Old Testament examples of imprisonment (Ezra 7:26) occurred after God's people had spent seventy years as captives in Babylon, where imprisonment was common. But under the law and system of government God ordained for Israel, long-term incarceration was not an option for punishment because it did not accomplish that purpose.

Americans in the late 1700s essentially imported from Europe the concept of a prison system. In fact, it was Quaker pacifists who first introduced the idea that, if incarcerated, criminals would become "penitent" (thus the name *penitentiary* for some facilities). But imprisonment in the United States has historically not worked as a means of punishment, nor has it effectively produced penitence. Sadly, the country now has the dual distinction of having the highest per capita number of inmates in the Western world and the highest crime rate.

The modern prison environment encourages brutality, homosexuality, and many other kinds of crime and sinful behavior. There is no way for inmates to make restitution for their offenses, and therefore they seldom regain a sense of dignity by spending years behind bars. And it is sad to say that most who serve sentences and are released sooner or later land back in prison.

"Because the sentence against an evil work is not executed speedily, therefore the heart of the sons of men is fully set in them to do evil" (Ecclesiastes 8:11). How much more are people "fully set . . . to do evil" when scriptural punishment is not administered at all? Thus, simply stated, the prison system as we know it is not a proper deterrent to or punishment for crime.

The history of Israel demonstrates what will happen to a nation that allows many bloody crimes to go unpunished. Partly for that sinful neglect God sent His chosen nation into captivity in Babylon. Through the prophet Ezekiel He prophesied such judgment on Israel: "Make a chain, for the land is filled with crimes of blood, and the city is full of violence. Therefore I will bring the worst of the Gentiles, and they will possess their houses; I will cause the pomp of the strong to cease, and their holy places shall be defiled" (Ezekiel 7:23–24). When the leaders of a nation fail to administer justice, they and their people fall under God's justice.

Today there is potentially a frightening parallel to the Jews' predicament of centuries ago. The United States and other supposedly sophisticated, technologically advanced societies have sanctioned abortion, which is nothing less than the murder of unborn children. Those who for nearly thirty years have encouraged this ghastly execution of the most defenseless and harmless of people created in God's image will not escape His eventual judgment. The blood of many millions of slaughtered babies cries out for justice, and God will provide it in His perfect timing.

Conscience

Realizing and understanding God's purposes for human government is another powerful incentive for us to obey civil authority. It's clear that those who don't submit to the laws and requirements of their community or nation make themselves vulnerable to punishment. And that's true for believers as well. But the New Testament indicates we ought to look toward a loftier motivation for good citizenship. Paul first indicates this truth in Romans 13:5, "Therefore you must be subject, not only because of wrath but also for conscience' sake." Then the apostle Peter essentially declares that, for Christians, to behave according to conscience is to order their lives for the sake of God's will. Conscience is His means of prompting us to respect and uphold His purposes for government: "Therefore submit yourselves to every ordinance of man for the Lord's sake, whether to the king as supreme, or to governors, as to those who are sent by him for the punishment of evildoers and for the praise of those who do good. For this is the will of God, that by doing good you may put to silence the ignorance of foolish men" (1 Peter 2:13–15).

Chapter 4

———◦《◉》◦———

Our Tax Obligation

*While many people—believers and unbelievers—view the
governments of contemporary democracies as corrupt and
unjust, by comparison the Roman government of
the first century was pagan, despotic, and often ruthless.*

Chapter 4

Our Tax Obligation

When April 15 nears, do you dread having to file a tax return? All Americans do, yet taxes are an important part of everyday life and vital for the functioning of governments in modern, highly developed countries. Taxes, especially income taxes, are also an annual source of irritation for many citizens who wonder why they're so high and why they're sometimes spent so foolishly. In the past, certain Christian groups have formally protested against what they perceived as tax abuse—the use of some tax monies in ways that seemed unbiblical or unconstitutional.

Certainly the authorities do not fairly spend every portion of properly levied taxes. But that does not justify tax evasion by citizens, especially believers. It is right for us to take advantage of legal deductions and other tax benefits, but we should never be looking for more ways to avoid paying taxes. Such attempts are usually at best unethical and at worst unlawful. Scripture commands that we obey the government's tax laws just as we do all other legitimate requirements.

While many people—believers and unbelievers—view the governments of contemporary democracies as corrupt and unjust, by comparison the Roman government of the first century was pagan, despotic, and often ruthless. Some emperors claimed deity for themselves and demanded worship from all their subjects. In its final years the Roman Empire deteriorated into a huge welfare state in which those people who still worked had to pay increasingly greater taxes to support the growing number who no longer worked. Roman officials also used a portion of their tax revenue to support pagan religious activity throughout the Empire, a practice that greatly concerned Christian and Jewish citizens of Rome.

In the outlying regions of the Empire, nationals of the area were appointed as tax collectors and assigned specific annual collection goals by Rome. Yet they were bound by no government restrictions that prevented them from exacting taxes as often as they wanted and at whatever exorbitant rate they pleased. Revenue that the tax agents gathered in excess of their goals simply stayed in their pockets. Such a system produced widespread abuse and resulted in much hatred and contempt of the tax collectors by their fellow countrymen. Those attitudes prevailed in Israel among the Jews (see Matthew 9:10–11).

That difficult situation provided the backdrop out of which the apostle Paul's teaching on the believer's tax-paying obligation emerged. He presents in two brief verses the rationale for our meeting this obligation: "For because of this you also pay taxes, for they are God's ministers attending continually to this very thing. Render therefore to all their due: taxes to whom taxes are due, customs to whom customs, fear to whom fear, honor to whom honor" (Romans 13:6–7).

BIBLE-TIME TAXES

Payment of taxes is definitely part of the Christian's general obligation to obey human authority. Paul's concise discussion of the tax situation flows naturally from his first five verses of Romans 13.

The Greek word for "taxes" in Romans 13:6 most commonly referred to a combination income and property tax paid by individuals, especially those who were citizens of a nation controlled by a foreign power. Of course, those were the circumstances for most in Paul's audience. The context suggests, however, that the apostle used the term to refer to all kinds of taxes—all of which Christians must pay.

Early Taxes

With his thorough knowledge of the Old Testament, Paul also was teaching with an awareness of the Jews' long experience with taxation. And that experience included the same kinds of oppressive and unjust taxes that God's people in the Roman Empire faced. During Nehemiah's leadership and the rebuilding of Jerusalem's walls, the people complained about the heavy taxes levied by the Persians: "We have borrowed money for the king's tax on our lands and vineyards. Yet now . . . it is not in our power to redeem them, for other men have our lands and vineyards" (Nehemiah 5:4–5).

Sometimes the unjust tax burden was levied by Israel's own kings. The northern tribes petitioned Rehoboam, the new

WHY GOVERNMENT CAN'T SAVE YOU

king, following the death of his father, Solomon: "Your father made our yoke heavy; now therefore, lighten the burdensome service of your father, and his heavy yoke which he put on us, and we will serve you" (1 Kings 12:4). But Rehoboam rejected their request and actually raised taxes. "He spoke to them according to the advice of the young men, saying, 'My father made your yoke heavy, but I will add to your yoke'" (verse 14). That terribly inequitable tax policy was the primary reason the northern tribes revolted against Rehoboam and established a separate Jewish state (see verses 16–20).

Sometimes the Jewish monarchs had to tax their people so the king could pay his tribute money (in essence, extortion) to an overlord nation. That's what occurred when Jehoiakim of Judah "taxed the land to give money according to the command of Pharaoh; he exacted the silver and gold from the people of the land, from every one according to his assessment, to give it to Pharaoh Necho" (2 Kings 23:35).

Scripture first mentions taxes in the record of the great Middle East famine during Joseph's time, when he became prime minister of Egypt. After he accurately interpreted Pharaoh's dreams as symbolically indicating seven years of abundance followed by seven years of famine, Joseph proposed that the nation set aside a fifth of the grain from the abundant period. "Then that food shall be as a reserve for the land for the seven years of famine which shall be in the land of Egypt, that the land may not perish during the famine" (Genesis 41:36; see also verses 48–49).

When the region suffered another famine some years later, Joseph—by then second only to Pharaoh over all of Egypt—made the 20 percent crop payment to the government an annual legal requirement (Genesis 47:26). Because of the unique insight and direct guidance the Lord gave Joseph, it's reasonable to infer that the 20 percent tax standard was divinely sanctioned, if not divinely authored.

Jewish Tax System

When God called His chosen people out of Egypt and created the nation of Israel, He also established a detailed tax system for the Jews. It was composed of a series of three tithes or 10 percent taxes plus three other taxes. The first tithe (Levites' tithe) went toward theocratic Israel's government expenses (Leviticus 27:30; see Numbers 18:21–24). The second tithe (festival tithe) paid for the development of a national religious, cultural, and social life, all of which fostered national unity (see Deuteronomy 12:10–19). The third tithe, which was collected only every third year and hence equaled a 3.3 percent annual tax, paid for welfare services (Deuteronomy 14:29).

The other three taxes were either prescribed at a smaller amount (the half-shekel tax) or administered more indirectly. The half-shekel tax, levied annually just on Israelite males, helped support the tabernacle and temple (see Exodus 30:14). The first indirect tax involved leaving some crops unharvested at the end of every season so that the poor could glean what was left (Leviticus 19:10). The second indirect tax dictated that every seventh year the people not cultivate the land. That produce which grew on its own was to be left for the poor, and whatever else remained was for the livestock to eat.

All six of those taxes, each of which was mandatory, added up to a yearly tax rate of 24 percent, slightly higher than the rate originated by Joseph in Egypt. (For a fuller discussion of

Old Testament tithes and taxes, see chapter 7 of my book *Whose Money Is It, Anyway?* [Nashville: Word, 2000]).

Taxes During Jesus' Day

By the time of Jesus' earthly ministry, the tax situation for the Jews was very different from what it was in the Old Testament era. They had experienced new and different forms of tax abuse and oppression, first during the Exile, then under Greek rule, and finally at the hands of Rome. The Romans did, however, allow Israel to collect certain religious taxes, such as the two-drachma temple tax. Jesus always taught that His followers should pay that tax *and* fulfill their obligations to the more secular taxes. Our Lord demonstrated His consistency on this topic, both to the disciples and before His unbelieving opponents.

Among a number of other issues, Christ's enemies foolishly sought to use the issue of paying taxes as a way to trap Him into revealing what they assumed were the true sentiments of an anti-establishment radical. Then they could use select anti-tax statements to charge Him with sedition against Rome and get those authorities to support His execution.

Toward the end of His ministry, Jesus' foes, led by the Pharisees, attempted once and for all to convict Him of some capital offense. In a memorable confrontation, the fiercely nationalistic Pharisees and the normally pro-Roman Herodians joined in their mutual hatred of Jesus to seek a way of charging Him with treason. The Pharisees knew that, as religious Jews who hated Rome, any unilateral charge they leveled at Jesus would be dismissed by the Romans as mere religious in-fighting among Jews. Therefore the Pharisees collaborated with the

Herodians, whom they normally refused to work with, to fashion an accusation that the authorities would more likely accept. If the Herodians backed a charge of treason against a prominent Jewish teacher like Jesus, the Pharisees felt more confident the Romans would consider the indictment credible.

Matthew's gospel records the scene this way:

> Then the Pharisees went and plotted how they might entangle Him in His talk. And they sent to Him their disciples with the Herodians, saying, "Teacher, we know that You are true, and teach the way of God in truth; nor do You care about anyone, for You do not regard the person of men. Tell us, therefore, what do You think? Is it lawful to pay taxes to Caesar, or not?" But Jesus perceived their wickedness, and said, "Why do you test Me, you hypocrites? Show Me the tax money." So they brought Him a denarius. And He said to them, "Whose image and inscription is this?" They said to Him, "Caesar's." And He said to them, "Render therefore to Caesar the things that are Caesar's, and to God the things that are God's." When they had heard these words, they marveled, and left Him and went their way. (Matthew 22:15–22)

The representatives of the Pharisees and Herodians cynically flattered the Lord by calling Him "Teacher" and hypocritically commended His personal and doctrinal integrity. Their real motive, however, was to spring a trap on Him while He dropped His guard and momentarily reveled in their man-centered praise. They assumed that like most people His ego would trip Him up and He would respond with the type of incriminating answer they sought. But Jesus, as God's Son, displayed divinely shrewd wisdom and discernment in answering their question on taxes.

The specific tax referred to was a poll tax. Sometimes called a head or census tax, it was to the Jews the most oner-ous assessment the Romans laid on them and was payable each year by every individual (see Luke 2:1–4). The religious Jews resented it so much because they felt they were God's personal properties, not Caesar's. Judas of Galilee led a revolt against the poll tax in A.D. 6. His rallying cry was that because God was Lord, the Jews could not and would not pay the poll tax to Rome. But his insurgency failed (Acts 5:37) and led to the decades-long Zealot movement against Rome, a cam-paign that itself eventually ceased with the Roman destruction of Jerusalem in A.D. 70.

So it was no accident that Christ's enemies put Him on the spot concerning the poll tax. If He supported the tax, the average Jewish man or woman who heretofore admired Him would turn against Him and perhaps that could hasten His execution. And if Jesus spoke out against the tax, the Pharisees and Herodians could report Him to the Romans for His insurrectionist tendencies.

However, our Lord's omniscience perceived their wicked-ness immediately (see John 2:25) and deflected their trick question with exactly the right strategy. He asked His oppo-nents to bring Him one of the coins used for the tax, and they handed Him a Roman denarius, which was a silver coin minted expressly by the emperor with his image on one side and an identifying inscription on the other.

Then Jesus asked them a very obvious and straightforward question, "Whose image and inscription is this?" The delegation from the Pharisees and Herodians quickly told Him it was Caesar's, figuring to hear Jesus, as the self-proclaimed Son of God, launch into a denunciation of the blasphemous Roman ruler. They no doubt presumed that their treachery was about to succeed.

But Jesus confounded His enemies' hopes and plans with this simple but profound reply: "Render therefore to Caesar the things that are Caesar's, and to God the things that are God's." "Render" in the original Greek means to give back or pay back, connoting a debt. Along with that is the notion of responsibility and obligation for something that's mandatory. Essentially, Jesus answered the group's question, "Is it lawful to pay taxes to Caesar, or not?" by telling them, "It is completely legitimate and the right thing to do to pay a tax to Caesar. After all, taxes belong under the government's jurisdiction."

It's significant that Jesus did not merely use the less forceful word *give* (translated "pay" in the New King James version) as the Pharisees had in their original question. They had a different choice of words because they saw Roman taxes as an illegitimate intrusion, which they would pay only with great reluctance. However, the Lord destroyed that position by declaring that the poll tax was legal *and* morally obligatory.

Christ's statement here is an assertion that citizens of all eras have a God-ordained obligation to pay taxes to their government. This duty is especially binding on Christians because they are servants of God's Word. As we saw in previous chapters, Scripture allows no exceptions or loopholes for disobeying government mandates just because you might live under a tyrannical or ungodly administration. The pagan government that crucified the Son of God still had a right to collect certain taxes, and its citizens had a legal and moral duty to pay them.

DIVINE RIGHT TO TAX

In the second half of Romans 13:6, the apostle Paul moves from the foundational principle that we should pay our taxes to an assertion that government has a divinely sanctioned prerogative to assess taxes: "for [rulers] are God's ministers attending continually to this very thing." Government leaders carry a larger responsibility than the unbelieving world or they themselves realize. No matter what position they have attained, what administrative competence they bring to the task, or what personal character qualities they possess, officials who assess and collect taxes are "God's ministers." The establishment and administration of a tax system derives from the legitimate set of duties that government authorities have as servants of God. That is reason enough for us to meet our tax obligations.

"Ministers" comes from the Greek *leitourgos,* which originally denoted a person who held public office at his own expense. Later the term referred to all officials, much the same way we use *public servant* today. Elsewhere the New Testament uses this word to refer to Paul himself ("a minister of Jesus Christ to the Gentiles," Romans 15:16), angels (Christ's "ministers," Hebrews 1:7), and even Jesus Christ ("a Minister of the sanctuary and of the true tabernacle," Hebrews 8:2). Most likely because of such usages and the fact that in the early church *leitourgos* came to designate any religious servant (minister of God), the term entered English vocabulary as *liturgy,* a prescribed religious service.

As a Pharisee (Philippians 3:5–6), every tax payment Paul had to make to support the hated Roman Empire certainly would have irritated him to the extreme. But following his conversion, the apostle was convinced he must submit to the God-ordained institution of government just as he submitted to the Lordship of Christ. And that submission included obedience to taxation, as well as to all aspects of government.

Paul's point in the conclusion of Romans 13:6 is clear. Because all public servants—from the most obscure to the most prominent, from the most despicable to the most honorable—who create and administer public policy are "God's ministers," we must obey their policies, including the unpopular duty of paying taxes. Even in determining tax rates and collection procedures, the authorities are attending, usually unwittingly, to one of their prerogatives and assisting in God's ministry—the orderly running of government.

THE CHRISTIAN'S OBLIGATION

In Romans 13:7, Paul summarizes the Christian's obligation to human government by enumerating several particulars involved in the tax-paying process and the spirit in which it should be done. "Render therefore to all their due: taxes to whom taxes are due, customs to whom customs, fear to whom fear, honor to whom honor."

First of all, the apostle reinforces Jesus' teaching in Matthew 22:21 by using the same Greek word *(apodidomi)*, "render," which we noted carries the idea of paying something already owed. Christians have both the moral and spiritual responsibility to pay taxes because that's what God requires of them. Anybody who dodges taxes or underreports what he or she owes is sinning against God as well as committing a crime against their government.

Paul is again referring to the onerous combination of

income taxes and property taxes that Rome demanded. The point is simply that believers must pay the variety of taxes (high and low) that might be due to various government officials and agencies. For us that might also involve the willing payment of such regular levies as the sales tax, utility taxes, in some countries the value-added tax, and assorted other occasional and one-time taxes (automobile, capital gains, inheritance). One such assessment Paul mentions in verse 7 is the custom, which is similar to the duty fee we must pay occasionally when we bring something of value into our country from abroad.

Paul summarizes his brief discourse on the believer's tax obligation by exhorting us concerning our attitude in fulfilling that duty. First he commands us to render "fear to whom fear" is due, which means having a genuine respect for those who rule us, even the ones responsible for tax collection. And he instructs us that such true respect must be accompanied by a sincere honor, or esteem. The respect and honor we pay to those who collect our taxes must be of the highest quality. Just because the whole process of filing and paying taxes (and enduring large withholdings from your paycheck) may be burdensome and distasteful, there is still absolutely no place for a hypocritical or cynical attitude toward our tax officials.

If Jesus and Paul taught believers to pay taxes, even during an era dominated by a pagan, oppressive government that openly persecuted Christians, then there is certainly no exemption from taxes for those of us who live in democracies. To argue that paying taxes to a secular, unbelieving government is somehow unspiritual or wrong is itself spurious and contradictory to the Word of God. All things belong to Him, but a certain amount of that wealth which He entrusts to each person must go to support the institutions of human government. That is in accord with the Lord's plan and decree and part of His perfect will for us.

Chapter 5

———◆◆◆———

Jesus' Lesson on Tax Exemptions

*If Jesus did not excuse Himself from paying taxes to the
"den of thieves" and "house of merchandise"
run by the proud, greedy, hypocritical Jewish religious leaders,
how much less can we shirk our duty to pay the taxes we owe?*

Chapter 5

Jesus' Lesson on Tax Exemptions

How do you learn best? Preferences vary from person to person. For some people the best way to learn a new concept or digest new information is simply to sit down and carefully read through pages of printed material. For others it's sufficient to take notes as someone else describes a process or explains a fresh idea. But for some of us the best way to thoroughly grasp an idea is to participate in or be an eyewitness to a practical application of the principle—and for these the teacher must provide a hands-on experience.

If someone would have asked the apostle Peter what learning style he preferred, he might well have said that the up-close, hands-on style was his favorite. That certainly would have fit his character as an action-oriented man of initiative. As his mentor and Lord, Christ knew exactly how best to convey the truth to Peter's heart and mind. And as the perfect teacher, Jesus wisely involved him directly and indirectly, in His miracles, parables, and sermons.

Jesus allowed Peter to experience a lesson firsthand in Matthew 17:24–27 on the importance of the believer's obedience to human government's tax demands. Interestingly, that lesson occurred right after Jesus gave the disciples another reminder that He would soon be delivered into the hands of the wicked authorities to die on the cross. In spite of the impending evil treatment He would suffer from the sinful religious and secular officials, our Lord wanted Peter and His followers to understand that they still must submit to government. And to make the lesson even more indelible and unforgettable, Jesus Himself would cooperate with the tax collector's requirements. If our Lord and Savior did not ignore or rebel against the tax laws of His day, neither can we flout our taxpaying duties today.

THE TEMPLE TAX

Peter was a well-known resident of the town of Capernaum, where other citizens also knew he was one of Jesus' leading disciples. With those facts in mind, the tax collectors singled out the disciple and confronted him with the issue of the temple tax during one of Jesus' final visits to Capernaum with the disciples: "When they had come to Capernaum, those who received the temple tax came to Peter and said, 'Does your Teacher not pay the temple tax?' He said, 'Yes'" (Matthew 17:24–25). (During this visit, Jesus may have been staying at Peter's house while the other eleven disciples lodged elsewhere, which would explain why only Peter and the Lord confronted the tax men in this particular episode.)

"Temple tax" derives from the single Greek word *didrachma,* which literally means "two drachmas," or "double drachma." It was a tax approved by the Romans so the Jews would have funds to operate the Jerusalem temple. The concept was essentially a continuation of an Old Testament tax, which was the half-shekel tax levied annually on every Israelite male twenty years old and older to provide for the maintenance and operation of the tabernacle in the wilderness. God mandated the assessment as follows: "This is what everyone among those who are numbered shall give: half a shekel according to the shekel of the sanctuary (a shekel is twenty gerahs). The half-shekel shall be an offering to the Lord. Everyone included among those who are numbered, from twenty years old and above, shall give an offering to the Lord" (Exodus 30:13–14). God further elaborated to Moses concerning the purpose of the tax: "You shall take the atonement money of the children of Israel, and shall appoint it for the service of the tabernacle of meeting, that it may be a memorial for the children of Israel before the Lord" (verse 16).

There was no such thing as a two-drachma coin in circulation, but the people in Jesus' time commonly used the term *didrachma* to denote the Jewish temple tax because two drachmas equaled the required half-shekel payment, which was approximately two days' pay for the typical worker.

The noted first-century Jewish historian Josephus wrote that, after the destruction of the temple in A.D. 70, Emperor Vespasian ordered the Jews throughout the Roman Empire to continue paying the annual two-drachma tax so that Rome could maintain the pagan temple of Jupiter Capitolinus. The ongoing tax also served as a harsh, vengeful reminder to Jews and every other nationality of the Empire of how expensive it was to oppose Rome.

Special tax collectors, not the usual Roman-appointed publicans, traveled throughout Palestine to begin gathering the taxes a month prior to the Passover due date for the assessments. Such men were the ones who confronted Peter with their question, "Does your Teacher not pay the temple tax?" That wording suggests a hostile tone, likely prompted by the Jewish leaders in Jerusalem who wanted to confront Christ and His closest followers on the issue of paying the tax. As we saw in chapter 4 with the Pharisees and Herodians and their confrontation with Jesus over the poll tax, the Lord's Jewish foes figured that because He claimed to be the Son of God He might also claim an exemption from or opposition to earthly taxes. If He did, they could pin a serious antigovernment charge against Him.

Peter, as a leader among the disciples, knew Jesus had consistently honored all tax requirements. Therefore he did not hesitate to answer the question himself with a simple and direct "Yes."

TAX SEMINAR 101

In the manner of most good teachers, Jesus preceded the illustrative portion of His lesson to Peter by establishing and explaining the principle behind His stories. He even did what ordinary teachers can merely attempt to do (and with only limited success)—He accurately anticipated what was on Peter's mind and what he needed to discuss and learn. To accomplish those ends, the Lord presented probably the shortest and most intriguing tax seminar ever devised.

As the disciple entered his house, presumably eager to tell Christ what had just happened outside, the Savior in His omniscience already was aware of what had occurred and what was said. We don't know precisely what Simon Peter's thoughts were, but Jesus' insightful comments to him reasonably imply that Peter wanted to know why the Son of God would condescend to pay taxes to people over whom He was eternally sovereign.

Jesus used the Socratic teaching method, common at that time in the Mediterranean world, to address Peter's unspoken question with a twofold question of His own, "And when he had come into the house, Jesus anticipated him, saying, 'What do you think, Simon? From whom do the kings of the earth take customs or taxes, from their sons or from strangers?'" (Matthew 17:25).

Nearly all governments at the time of Christ were autocratic, with all power resting in the hands of some imperial individual ("kings of the earth"). They all levied the two usual kinds of assessments ("customs" on goods and "taxes" [poll tax] on individuals) to fund their governments and support the royal family.

Jesus was asking a rhetorical question, and the obvious answer He expected was that it would be senseless for a father to collect revenue from the sons who depended on him. Such a father would in effect be taxing himself. Therefore it made much more sense that the king would tax strangers, or his subjects outside his royal family.

Peter quickly had the right answer to Jesus' question, and Jesus immediately made this concise summarization: "Then the sons are free" (verse 26). Under the monarchies of that time, members of the rulers' families ("sons") were exempt from taxation. If our Lord's brief conclusion were the end of His tax lesson, we could easily argue that, as children of God and fellow heirs with Christ, we ought not be liable for human tax obligations, either.

If there were any tax liability Christ could have claimed exemption from, it certainly would have been the temple tax. The temple was built to honor His Father and as a sanctuary for the presentation of offerings and sacrifices to Him. Jesus called the temple "My Father's house" (John 2:16; see Luke 2:49) and proclaimed Himself as "One greater than the temple" (Matthew 12:6). As God, He could have placed Himself above the burden of paying the temple tax, just as He could have avoided all earthly humiliation and persecution. But Jesus did not do any of that. Instead, He willingly set aside His divine glory, "taking the form of a bondservant, and coming in the likeness of men" (Philippians 2:7). In humbling Himself and taking on all the basic attributes of humanity (except sin), Christ willingly accepted the obligations and duties of a normal man, and that included paying His taxes.

No matter how unfair or unjustified a particular tax is or seems to be, the Son of God instructs His disciples (then and now) to pay it, even if the assessment is used wastefully, foolishly, and in other ways that do not honor God. If Jesus did not excuse Himself from paying taxes to the "den of thieves" and "house of merchandise" run by the proud, greedy, hypocritical Jewish religious leaders, how much less can we shirk our duty to pay the taxes we owe? When our Lord began the final part of His lesson to Peter with the admonition "lest we offend them," He clearly implied that the two of them were to willingly and without argument use the divine provision of tax money for its intended purpose—the temple tax.

GOD PROVIDES

The Bible has no record, other than Jesus' experiential lesson for Peter, that God miraculously supplied someone's tax payment. But on that occasion our Lord, in His sovereign omniscience and omnipotence, chose to work supernaturally to underscore the point that He was indeed the Son of God and did in fact have total control over the tax system. Even though He could have exercised His divine prerogative not to pay the temple tax, He willingly agreed to join Peter in paying the tax He owed. Here's how He instructed His disciple: "Go to the sea, cast in a hook, and take the fish that comes up first. And when you have opened its mouth, you will find a piece of money; take that and give it to them for Me and you" (Matthew 17:27).

Peter obeyed Jesus' command, and the events unfolded just as He said they would. The coin Peter extracted from the fish's mouth was a Roman *stater*. The stater equaled two didrachma, so it was the coin to use in paying the two drachma temple tax. It became customary for two Jewish men, such as Jesus and Peter, to pay their tax together, using a single stater. Thus the coin Peter found was precisely the amount of money needed to cover the tax payment for Jesus and himself.

The point of Jesus' lesson is clear. All believers must obey the requirements of the tax system under which they live. And God is there to provide the means—perhaps not as dramatically as for Peter, but nevertheless just as faithfully—for us to fulfill those obligations.

Undoubtedly Peter still had distinct memories of the unique lesson Christ gave him using the ordinary things of life when he exhorted his Christian readers about their extraordinary roles as citizens in an unbelieving world: "You are a chosen generation, a royal priesthood, a holy nation, His own special people, that you may proclaim the praises of Him who called you out of darkness into His marvelous light" (1 Peter 2:9). God has adopted into His family all of us who believe. We are His children and primarily citizens of His eternal kingdom. But until He calls us to heaven or returns in power and glory, we are also citizens of this world, with a mandate to minister as His priests to the unbelieving citizens around us. That high calling requires us to present an excellent testimony in all we do and say before the watching world. Peter goes on to say, "Beloved, I beg you as sojourners and pilgrims, abstain from fleshly lusts which war against the soul, having your conduct honorable among the Gentiles, that when they speak against you as evildoers, they may, by your good works which they observe, glorify God in the day of visitation" (verses 11–12).

Included in any testimony of model citizenship would certainly be faithful and consistent compliance with all the government's tax requirements. The people of the early church did not mount a tax revolt against the heavy tax burden assessed by the Roman Empire. Neither did they start an insurrection against the cruel and wicked—but in those days commonplace—institution of slavery. On the contrary, they obeyed the Holy Spirit, who transformed the terminology of slavery (slave, bond-slave, bondage, servant, etc.) into symbols of Christian dedication and submission.

So, although we are primarily citizens of God's kingdom (Ephesians 2:19; Philippians 3:17–21; Hebrews 12:22–23)— and we should rejoice in that privilege and make its reality our highest priority—that does not allow us to disregard our taxpaying responsibilities as citizens of various earthly nations. What our heavenly citizenship should remind us of is that we have a special obligation to taxes and all other aspects of human authority because, as we have already seen in this volume, God ordains each one for our well being.

By being faithful taxpayers, like the Lord Jesus and the apostle Peter, we show respect for God-ordained laws, even when we might not like them and know that they are often administered by leaders who are ungodly, corrupt, and oppressive. By obeying *all* the laws we demonstrate a love for God, for our country, and for our fellow citizens. Such a consistent testimony is much more likely to compel the unsaved to be drawn to the power that makes that lifestyle possible.

Chapter 6

Supporting Our Leaders: How and Why

What it all comes down to, I believe, is learning to be a faithful and consistent supporter of your government leaders, whoever they are, in whatever nation you reside.

Chapter 6

Supporting Our Leaders: How and Why

Our lives are filled with practical reminders each day: "I need to get up an hour earlier tomorrow." "One of our cars needs an oil change this week." "I need to finish my report for the sales conference before I do anything else at the office today." "Before I forget, I must send those recipes to my sister-in-law." And that's how life goes from week to week. Without our daily reminders, we would no doubt overlook some of our most essential tasks or appointments. Although we know in principle what we need to do and how we need to do it, if it were not for day-planner notebooks or the increasingly popular hand-held computer planners, many of us would forget our own birthdays. What's worse, we would disappoint, frustrate, or anger family, friends, and co-workers with our irresponsible planning.

Some people might even say you can't have too many

reminders concerning life's priorities. For them it's the only way to ensure that they complete an important project or the only method that helps them keep up with their daily priorities. Scripture and church history also teach us through the effective use of reminders, as we can see when it comes to our topic of the believer's continual submission to authority and respect for human government. Even though you may say, "I now have a good grasp on how I ought to view politics and government," you still must be concerned with how you as a Christian apply that understanding in the long term. What it all comes down to, I believe, is learning to be a faithful and consistent supporter of your government leaders, whoever they are, in whatever nation you reside.

LEADER SUPPORT
FROM EARLY CHRISTIANS

Respect for human leaders was the norm for the early church long before the Roman Empire was "Christianized." One example of the early Christians' righteous pattern of support for their ruling superiors is the following prayer composed by Clement of Rome near the end of the first century. Remarkably, this prayer was offered in the wake of severe persecutions ordered by the emperors Nero and Domitian:

> Guide our steps to walk in holiness and righteousness and singleness of heart, and to do those things that are good and acceptable in Thy sight, and in the sight of our rulers. Yes, Lord, cause Thy face to shine upon us in peace for our good, that we may be sheltered by Thy mighty hand and delivered from every sin by Thine

outstretched arm. Deliver us from those who hate us wrongfully. Give concord and peace to us and to all who dwell on earth, as Thou didst to our fathers, when they called on Thee in faith and truth with holiness, while we render obedience to Thine almighty and most excellent name, and to our earthly rulers and governors.

Thou, O Lord and Master, hast given them the power of sovereignty through Thine excellent and unspeakable might, that we, knowing the glory and honour which Thou hast given them, may submit ourselves to them, in nothing resisting Thy will. Grant them therefore, O Lord, health, peace, concord and stability, that they may without failure administer the government which Thou hast committed to them. For Thou, O heavenly Master, King of the ages, dost give to the sons of men glory and honour and power over all things that are in the earth. Do Thou, O Lord, direct their counsel according to what is good and acceptable in Thy sight, that they, administering in peace and gentleness with godliness the power which Thou hast committed to them, may obtain Thy favour.[1]

Prayers of Believers

In the second century Justin Martyr, church father and theologian, wrote this to the emperor Antoninus Pius, "Everywhere we [Christians], more readily than all men, endeavour to pay to those appointed by you the taxes both ordinary and extraordinary, as we have been taught by [Jesus]. . . . Whence to God alone we render worship, but in other things we gladly serve you, acknowledging you as kings and rulers of men, and praying that with your kingly power you be found to possess also sound judgment."[2]

A later church father, Tertullian, wrote concerning Rome, "Without ceasing, for all our emperors we offer prayer. We pray for life prolonged; for security to the empire; for protection to the imperial house; for brave armies, a faithful senate, a virtuous people, the world at rest, whatever, as man or Caesar, an emperor would wish."[3]

The remarkable thing about those statements is not the profundity of their sentiments as such, but that they were expressed in the midst of very difficult times for the church. It was attempting to survive and grow even though targeted for sometimes-vicious persecution by a pagan, cruel, anti-Christian government in Rome.

Accusations Against Believers

Most key Roman officials viewed Christians as simply members of a sect within Judaism. Therefore believers became targets of the same kind of slander and malicious rumors that the government had previously circulated about the Jews. For example, Apion made this false accusation against the Jews: "In the reign of Antiochus Epiphanes, the Jews every year fattened a Greek, and having solemnly offered him up as a sacrifice on a fixed day in a certain forest, ate his entrails and swore eternal hostility to the Greeks."[4]

The enemies of the church also accused Christians of insurrection against Rome and against all other human authority. That's what the Jewish leaders said about Jesus (John 19:15). Some charged believers with atheism simply because they refused to worship pagan gods, including Caesar.

Others distorted the scriptural teaching concerning the Lord's Table and said the followers of Christ were cannibals (see John 6:51–53; 1 Corinthians 10:16).

Perhaps the most incredible charge aimed at the early Christians was that they had incestuous relationships with one another. That originated because pagans heard believers referring to fellow believers as brothers and sisters in Christ. Unbelievers also distorted in a similar fashion the divine command to "greet one another with a holy kiss."

In the early decades of the church, believers were also accused of various other offenses. Unbelievers were upset because Christians supposedly ruined the trade in the idol-making industry (see Acts 19:21–41). Because some homes were divided when part of a family believed in Christ and another part did not, the pagans blamed believers for destroying family life. Then the church was accused of encouraging a slave rebellion within the Empire just because converted slaves received new life and dignity in Christ. And for refusal to adopt the world's lifestyle, believers were called antisocial.

A Godly Response

With God's help, the early church withstood that array of outrageous accusations and carried the gospel to every part of its world. Believers responded to relentless persecution with godly living, as 1 Peter 2:12 directs: "Having your conduct honorable among the Gentiles, that when they speak against you as evildoers, they may, by your good works which they observe, glorify God in the day of visitation." Such behavior left no ammunition for the ungodly to use in hurling false charges at Christians, and it served to attract the unsaved to Jesus Christ.

The situation is not that much different in our culture today. There is a general bias against the truth and righteousness that genuine Christianity stands for, but we as believers should nevertheless live as godly citizens who support the civil authorities. In complete agreement with Paul's earlier teaching, the apostle Peter charged his audience and us to "submit yourselves to every ordinance of man for the Lord's sake" (1 Peter 2:13).

We could also translate the command "submit yourselves" (from a military term for a soldier being under the authority of a superior) to read "put yourselves in an attitude of submission." The world has always associated that attitude with weakness and cowardice, but Scripture declares it to be the beginning foundation for our support of government leaders. "My son, fear the LORD and the king; do not associate with those given to change; for their calamity will rise suddenly, and who knows the ruin those two can bring?" (Proverbs 24:21–22). That kind of strong loyalty is always a proper component of good Christian citizenship.

CITIZEN REMINDERS

Reminders from the past and from Scripture are certainly instructive, and they provide plenty of incentive for us to please God as good citizens wherever He has placed us. But now the question arises, "Are there any reminders we need to bring before our civic officials that will demonstrate our support for them and indicate to them that we have their best interests at heart?" The answer is yes, so let's look at what God's Word has to say about the most important of such "godly citizen reminders."

Leadership Is a Divine Trust

First of all, Christians need to periodically remind their leaders that civil responsibilities are given to them from the supervising hand of God. An infallible source for the truth of that reminder is the Book of Psalms with its many declarations that God is sovereign over the affairs of mankind. Just two of those declarations are sufficient to make the point. "But You, LORD, are on high forevermore" (Psalm 92:8). "The LORD reigns, He is clothed with majesty; the Lord is clothed, He has girded Himself with strength. Surely the world is established, so that it cannot be moved. Your throne is established from of old; You are from everlasting" (93:1–2).

When Nebuchadnezzar of Babylon showed his disregard for this truth—"Is not this great Babylon, that I have built for a royal dwelling by my mighty power and for the honor of my majesty?" (Daniel 4:30)—God immediately judged the king's arrogant attitude of self-importance. "While the word was still in the king's mouth, a voice fell from heaven: 'King Nebuchadnezzar, to you it is spoken: the kingdom has departed from you! And they shall drive you from men, and your dwelling shall be with the beasts of the field. They shall make you eat grass like oxen; and seven times shall pass over you, until you know that the Most High rules in the kingdom of men, and gives it to whomever He chooses" (verses 31–32). When God's prophetic words were perfectly fulfilled, Nebuchadnezzar was constrained to acknowledge God's proper role, "At the end of the time I, Nebuchadnezzar, lifted my eyes to heaven, and my understanding returned to me; and I blessed the Most High and praised and honored Him who lives forever: for His dominion is an everlasting dominion, and His kingdom is from generation to generation" (verse 34).

God Is the Ultimate and Only Sovereign

Emerging logically from the fact that human leadership is a divine trust is the truth that God is sovereign over this world and all its governments. From time to time as appropriate, we should respectfully remind our government authorities that God "disciplines nations" (Psalm 94:10, NIV), and that some day "He is coming to judge the earth. With righteousness He shall judge the world, and the peoples with equity" (Psalm 98:9). As God's people, Christians should "declare His glory among the nations, His wonders among all peoples. For the LORD is great and greatly to be praised; He is to be feared above all gods. For all the gods of the peoples are idols, but the LORD made the heavens" (Psalm 96:3–5).

The founders and leaders of any good government will recognize the presence of God in the process and will not dare to exclude His principles from the conduct of governing. Whenever leadership is detached from God and is indifferent to or ignorant of His sovereignty, justice suffers and the overall effectiveness and efficiency of government is severely diminished, often to the point of corruption. Obviously, such a situation ought to be the last thing we as believers want for our nation.

Leaders Have Civic Duties

Another reminder that proves we are truly supportive of our leaders is the one that affirms we will choose only those who are faithful to all their governing responsibilities. Once rulers know that they serve only because a sovereign God has allowed them to, they should understand that He is holding them accountable to serve society responsibly and properly (see Amos 2:4; Jonah 1:2). And that accountability includes a number of areas for which we can give our leaders four specific reminders.

1. *God requires humility.* Humility is perhaps the least common character trait that government officials display. There is a great temptation and tendency toward pride for those who wield power and have influence over important legislation. But the Lord promises this: "I will halt the arrogance of the proud, and will lay low the haughtiness of the terrible" (Isaiah 13:11). Therefore, it's important that we not let our leaders forget the wisdom of shunning pride and striving after humility.

2. *God demands justice, mercy, and compassion.* A second important area of good governing that we ought to regularly remind our leaders of encompasses the key virtues of justice, mercy, and compassion. When an unidentified ruler of Babylon did not display these qualities, the Lord judged him harshly: "How the oppressor has ceased, the golden city ceased! The Lord has broken the staff of the wicked, the scepter of the rulers; he who struck the people in wrath with a continual stroke, he who ruled the nations in anger, is persecuted and no one hinders. . . .Your pomp is brought down to Sheol, and the sound of your stringed instruments; the maggot is spread under you, and worms cover you" (Isaiah 14:4–6, 11).

3. *God calls for enforcement of the law.* It is entirely legitimate that we remind those in authority that God is expecting them to preserve order by fair and firm law enforcement. The Old Testament again contains sobering reminders of what

happened to past rulers who did not enforce existing laws. When Judah's King Zedekiah failed to punish the slaveholders who mistreated their slaves, God judged him and his officials for their dereliction of duty (Jeremiah 34:12–22). Robert D. Culver makes this accurate analysis of what lax law enforcement leads to:

> Where theistic religion grows weak, [the concept of justice] will weaken. Crimes then are defined as antisocial activity, which in turn is then merely what the majority says it is. Then punishments seem to be the result of the majorities ganging up on the minority. This in turn seems inconsistent with democratic feelings. The result is a decline in uniform application of penalties for crime, resultant miscarriage of justice, trampling on the rights of law-abiding people, together with an increase in what ought to be called crime.[5]

4. *God opposes selfish oppression.* We also ought to remind our government leaders that God does not want them to seek their own welfare at the expense of their constituents. Here's how God, through the prophet Jeremiah, warned the oppressive Shallum, son of King Josiah:

> "Woe to him who builds his house by unrighteousness and his chambers by injustice, who uses his neighbor's service without wages and gives him nothing for his work, who says, 'I will build myself a wide house with spacious chambers, and cut out windows for it, paneling it with cedar and painting it with vermilion.' Shall you reign because you enclose yourself in cedar? Did

not your father eat and drink, and do justice and righteousness? Then it was well with him. He judged the
cause of the poor and needy; then it was well. Was not
this knowing Me?" says the Lord. "Yet your eyes and
your heart are for nothing but your covetousness, for
shedding innocent blood, and practicing oppression
and violence." (Jeremiah 22:13–17)

Officials are not to emulate Shallum, but instead they should
empathize with citizens' needs and extend kindness to them
by actually relieving suffering and want. God wants them to
be more like King Josiah, who practiced "justice and righteousness" and cared about "the cause of the poor and needy"
(verses 15–16).

Although we as believers have a duty to submit to civil
authority, it is also biblical for us to remind leaders of their
own duty to fulfill all their God-ordained responsibilities and
rule according to the broad plan of His will.

SUPPORTING OUR LEADERS: THE FINAL PRODUCT

For a good team in athletics, the route to a winning game or
a successful season may at times bear little resemblance to the
final destination. For the players, there will sometimes be dis-
couragement when the team falls behind in a game or slides
into a brief losing streak. They might be tempted to abandon
fundamental techniques, when those no longer appear effective, in favor of some novel approach that will "shake things
up." For the team's fans, there will also be times of frustration
and impatience as they witness the players' various struggles.

Some fans will even want to quit supporting the team altogether, or at least until the players and coaches can finally pull together as a team.

Our efforts to be good and godly citizens in a fallen world often produce feelings that mirror those of athletes and fans in the sports realm. Our leaders frequently do not appreciate our most conscientious attempts to support and obey their government. As the moral and ethical climates in our national cultures and administrations grow worse and worse, the temptation for us is to call our efforts useless and look for some new approaches. Too often that can lead us to conclude, "Maybe support of my government really doesn't matter, or a little disobedience of wicked authority is justified after all." But we as Christians know that the expedient way is not God's way and that we need to persevere in doing what's right. His Word offers us three clear guidelines that will produce a God-honoring final product of support for our leaders.

The Real Battle Is a Spiritual One

The greatest support we can render for those men and women who rule over us is to persist in working for the good of society with spiritual weapons. We need to remind ourselves often of the truth we noted in chapter one of this book, the apostle Paul's declaration that believers are ultimately engaged in spiritual warfare: "For though we walk in the flesh, we do not war according to the flesh. For the weapons of our warfare are not carnal but mighty in God for pulling down strongholds, casting down arguments and every high thing that exalts itself against the knowledge of God, bring-

ing every thought into captivity to the obedience of Christ"
(2 Corinthians 10:3–5).

That passage pictures an army advancing on a fortress and
destroying it. The Holy Spirit commands us to conquer with
divinely powered spiritual weapons that will demolish or tear
down immense strongholds. These strongholds and fortresses
are defined as "arguments and every high thing," meaning
ideologies, religions, worldviews, philosophies, psychologies,
and theories that are exalted "against the knowledge of God."
The language is describing any and every anti-God, thus
anti-biblical, idea invented by demons and men. And only
the power of divine truth will defeat those false ideologies.
So, as believers, we attack with the Scriptures the lying theories that oppose God's truth. That is the sole way we can
rescue the victims of those lies and bring them to Christ.

When Paul says we are to be "bringing every thought into
captivity to the obedience of Christ" he is picturing a soldier
using a spear to take prisoners of war. All opinions and
philosophies that oppose God must eventually bow in obedience to Jesus Christ. If we adequately arm ourselves with the
sword of Scripture (Ephesians 6:17) and keep ourselves in a
continual attitude of prayer (1 Thessalonians 5:17), not only
our government leaders but our fellow citizens will be awak-
ened to the bankruptcy of unbiblical ideas and to their need
for repentance. As a result, some will be set free for salvation
in Christ (see Isaiah 55:11; 1 Timothy 2:1–6).

We Must Live Responsibly

As Christians, we are no longer enslaved to the sinful world
system because Christ's death on the cross has redeemed us

(1 Peter 1:18–19). When the apostle Peter discusses our submission to human government, he writes that we should operate as persons who are "free, yet not using liberty as a cloak for vice, but as bondservants of God" (1 Peter 2:16). We are not to use our liberty in Christ as a rationalization for engaging in sin. Therefore any appeal to a "higher law" to justify disobeying or ignoring laws we don't like is sinful.

We are free to obey and serve the Lord, not merely ourselves (1 Corinthians 7:22; Galatians 5:13; see Romans 6:22), which includes obeying all He commands regarding the support of our civil officials. Our citizenship in heaven and our Christian liberty should encourage us all the more to be good and supportive citizens of the earthly nations God has placed us in.

Supporting Our Leaders Brings Benefits

First Peter 2:17 lists, by way of command, four beneficial aspects that result from our support of authority: "Honor all people. Love the brotherhood. Fear God. Honor the king." If we are submitting to and honoring the government, other individual citizens who were created in the image of God (see James 3:9) also will be honored and respected. We might not agree with others' positions or activities, but if we're good citizens and neighbors, we will respect other people as persons God has made. Of course, such respect should easily extend to love for other Christians ("the brotherhood").

When we give proper support to earthly government it demonstrates that we "fear God" and trust Him no matter how difficult and discouraging it is to live in an ungodly society. It shows others that we reverence Him as the Sovereign who is working all things according to His perfect plan.

Finally, and most obviously, our support for our leaders will bring additional honor and respect to them ("honor the king"). And that, along with the other three benefits, gives credibility to our Christian testimony.

Concerning the believer's role in this vital matter of support for his or her government leaders, Culver again provides us with an insightful commentary on the rationale for our behavior: "The Christian serves his country, obeys its laws, and supports its rulers so far as a biblically informed conscience lets him, not out of servile fear or out of rigid, dogmatic necessity, but because he knows it is right. Right (understood as expression of the will of the Creator-God) is ultimately the ground of all righteous action."[6] When you do what is right in these matters, you "let your light so shine before men, that they may see your good works and glorify your Father in heaven" (Matthew 5:16).

Chapter 7

Daniel's Uncompromising Civil Service

Daniel's steady and godly performance in the arena of politics and government is an amazing testimony to the truth that God's sovereignty works in mysterious yet perfect harmony with man's responsibility.

Chapter 7

Daniel's Uncompromising Civil Service

There is no better Old Testament example than Daniel of one who had an ideal relationship with secular authority—he maintained his walk as a believer and his life as a responsible citizen in perfect harmony. He is the rare example of one whose career was primarily devoted to statesmanship and civil service, yet without any of the modern negative connotations of being "a politician." Today Daniel's name is synonymous with integrity and quality of service, the model servant who was loyal to his government superiors, but not at the expense of his scriptural convictions.

Daniel was certainly recognized by his contemporaries as a superb role model. One of those men was the prophet Ezekiel, who through the Holy Spirit listed Daniel as one of the great men of righteousness of all time (Ezekiel 14:14). Actually, Ezekiel mentioned just three men, and two of them

WHY GOVERNMENT CAN'T SAVE YOU

(Noah and Job) were already dead. Rarely does a living person receive such distinguished mention, so Daniel had to be an exceptional man, undoubtedly one whose actions and attitudes are worth studying and emulating.

THE ADVANTAGE OF GOOD PREPARATION

Daniel's rise to prominence began during a difficult period for God's people. He was among the many Jewish young men whom Babylon's King Nebuchadnezzar took hostage after the first Babylonian invasion of Judah in 606 B.C. After Judah was finally defeated and its period of captivity in Babylon began in 586 B.C., Daniel and some of his peers were groomed to assist Nebuchadnezzar's long-range plans for world domination.

Daniel 1:3–4 describes in part the kind of men the Babylonians were seeking for government service: "Then the king instructed Ashpenaz, the master of his eunuchs, to bring some of the children of Israel and some of the king's descendants and some of the nobles, young men in whom there was no blemish, but good-looking, gifted in all wisdom, possessing knowledge and quick to understand, who had ability to serve in the king's palace, and whom they might teach the language and literature of the Chaldeans [Babylonians]."

Daniel and his companions, by the simple fact that they were selected, proved that they were already well qualified for public service. First, they were "gifted in all wisdom"—they were already familiar with many academic subjects and would rather easily be able to learn new ones. Second, they were "possessing knowledge and quick to understand," which means they could use discernment, correlate facts, and draw logical conclusions. In summary, Daniel and the other young men had quality educational backgrounds and good potential, which prepared them well for serving with excellence in their new country and relating properly to the demands of their government.

OBEDIENCE WITHOUT COMPROMISE

Daniel 1:4 concludes by saying "whom they might teach the language and literature of the Chaldeans [Babylonians]." That indicates that Daniel would have to engage in a new education curriculum, one that would contain some different and challenging subjects from what he studied in Judah. Daniel's reeducation process included both positive and negative aspects. Although it was probably helpful for him to acquire the latest information in science, math, and linguistics, at the same time he had to be extremely discerning to deal with other subjects that the Babylonians required, such as astrology, mythology, and their distinctive brands of polytheism. With divine help, Daniel was agreeable only up to a certain point with Babylon's indoctrination course and the demands of his civil service superiors. And God did give him the courage and conviction to support and obey his government, yet without compromising biblical standards or abandoning his role as God's servant.

The Babylonian officials finished up their training program for Daniel and friends by providing servings of the best and most sumptuous royal food and beverage. This was another calculated attempt by Nebuchadnezzar's court to win over the Hebrew youth to the lifestyle and advantages of upper-level Babylonian officials. Perhaps if the trainees experienced certain perks and luxuries accompanying their new positions they would be more loyal to Babylon and less inclined to cling to former customs. But Daniel didn't accept that clever line of reasoning, opting instead for an uncompromising, scriptural resolve to do the right thing, not whatever was expedient. "But Daniel purposed in his heart that he would not defile himself with the portion of the king's delicacies, nor with the wine which he drank; therefore he requested of the chief of the eunuchs that he might not defile himself" (Daniel 1:8).

Daniel took a firm stand on the issue of food and drink for two reasons. First, he was well aware that God's Law had set forth very specific dietary restrictions for His followers (see Leviticus 7:23–27; 11:1–47; Deuteronomy 12:15–28; 14:1–29).

Second, Daniel had to refuse the king's menu because he knew the fancy food and wine had initially been dedicated to Babylon's false gods. And the Old Testament commanded the Jews not to engage in any forms of idolatry: "You shall have no other gods before Me. You shall not make for yourself a carved image, or any likeness of anything that is in heaven above, or that is in the earth beneath, or that is in the water under the earth; you shall not bow down to them nor serve them. For I the Lord your God, am a jealous God" (Exodus 20:3–5; see also Leviticus 19:4; Deuteronomy 5:7–8). To partake of any of those foods or beverages would have been the same as Daniel's participation in an idolatrous pagan feast.

Daniel's uncompromising stance regarding dietary matters reminds us again of how we sometimes must relate to our leaders: at times we will have to refuse obedience if such compliance would violate God's will. We must not compromise on an issue if His Word does not allow us to do so. If authorities ask us to do something that is contrary to Scripture, we must side with Scripture and respectfully decline to obey.

Many believers today find it difficult or intimidating to know just how to react when faced with a situation parallel to Daniel's. They hesitate on doing what's right and then give in to the authorities' unbiblical demand. Or they hold true to biblical principles and refuse to obey the sinful demand but do so in a way that does not make their godly convictions clear. (Or they might express the reasons for their refusal to comply *too clearly*, employing a very blunt, self-righteous, and unloving manner.) But none of those extremes was present in Daniel's interaction with his government superiors.

Instead, several facets were evident in his lifestyle that highlighted his uncompromising integrity, coupled with loving graciousness and tact.

Daniel Made the Issues Clear

Daniel was transparent with Ashpenaz and made his position on dietary restrictions clear right away: "He requested of the chief of the eunuchs that he might not defile himself" (Daniel 1:8). Daniel underscored the unambiguousness of his beliefs by using the term "defile," which is a strong word whose Old Testament usage always indicated something that was an abomination to God. Synonyms Daniel could have used are "contaminate," "corrupt," "pollute," and "adulterate."

Daniel wanted to make sure the Babylonians did not misunderstand his position on the issue at hand. Therefore he undoubtedly compared and contrasted Jewish food requirements with the Babylonian royal menu and carefully set into perspective his deep concerns about idolatry.

Unlike so many people, Daniel heeded the warning of Proverbs 29:25, "The fear of man brings a snare," and did not allow the dictates of others, even his leaders, to deter him. He, like other great men of Scripture, believed that "whoever trusts in the Lord shall be safe" (verse 25). David, for example, made it crystal clear where he stood on the crucial issues of life: "I have proclaimed the good news of righteousness in the great assembly; indeed, I do not restrain my lips, O LORD, You Yourself know. I have not hidden Your righteousness within my heart; I have declared Your faithfulness and Your salvation; I have not concealed Your lovingkindness and Your truth from the great assembly" (Psalm 40:9–10).

In the New Testament, the apostle Paul encourages a similar attitude for the life of the Christian: "Only let your conduct be worthy of the gospel of Christ, so that whether I come and see you or am absent, I may hear of your affairs, that you stand fast in one spirit, with one mind, striving together for the faith of the gospel, and not in any way terrified by your adversaries" (Philippians 1:27–28; see 2 Timothy 1:7–8).

Daniel Was Committed to Spiritual Excellence

As Daniel dealt with officials in the royal court, he was also careful to operate from a standard of personal and spiritual excellence, one that exceeded routine expectations. "So Daniel said to the steward . . . 'Please test your servants for ten days, and let them give us vegetables to eat and water to drink'" (Daniel 1:11–12).

Most people in Daniel's day, as is still true today, were not vegetarians. But Daniel and his friends were willing to eat beans and seed if that extraordinary behavior would free them from the requirement to obey the king's wishes concerning food.

In addition to adopting the more stringent standard of vegetarianism, Daniel decided not to drink wine at all, much less the king's wine. That decision further demonstrated his determination to set a high standard. It also revealed that Daniel was committed to personal sacrifice if that would ensure a healthy relationship with official authority.

Daniel's dedication to excellence of character and his willingness to sacrifice certain privileges to remain beyond compromise with his leaders sets a splendid example for us.

In all our interaction with civil authority, we should strive, with God's help, to act from a foundation of unwavering excellence—spiritually, morally, and ethically.

Daniel Was Rewarded for His Stand

God is pleased with those who live by His standards of righteousness, as established in His Word, in whatever arena they find themselves. "The righteous shall flourish like a palm tree, he shall grow like a cedar in Lebanon. Those who are planted in the house of the LORD shall flourish in the courts of our God. They shall bear fruit in old age; they shall be fresh and flourishing" (Psalm 92:12–14).

Daniel proves that whenever one relates well to his government—and even serves in it with excellence—he will flourish and receive the Lord's blessing. And he experienced such blessing in the form of acceptance from Nebuchadnezzar's court even before he made his dietary request: "Now God had brought Daniel into the favor and goodwill of the chief of the eunuchs" (Daniel 1:9).

That is an encouraging reminder that God's sovereignty encompasses governmental activities and the thoughts, feelings, and actions of rulers. Proverbs 21:1 declares, "The king's heart is in the hand of the LORD, like the rivers of water; He turns it wherever He wishes." The blessing Daniel received in the Babylonian court also authenticates another of the Lord's Old Testament promises: "When a man's ways please the LORD, He makes even his enemies to be at peace with him" (Proverbs 16:7). If we are consistently faithful as good citizens and at the same time uncompromising and obedient to God's requirements when they supersede our government's, God also will uphold us and bless us. But if we don't emulate Daniel's wise and balanced approach of godly citizenship, it's easy to forget God's faithfulness. However, the psalmist reminds us, "For [Israel's] sake He remembered His covenant, and relented according to the multitude of His mercies. He also made them to be pitied by all those who carried them away captive" (Psalm 106:45–46).

Joseph (Genesis 39:1–4) and Moses (Hebrews 11:23–29) also learned to appreciate and trust in the Lord's blessings and protection as they lived for Him in the challenging contexts of hostile governments and unfamiliar cultures. God's faithfulness is still available to us as we seek to fulfill our responsibilities toward increasingly more unfriendly and insensitive national and local governments. Our duty is simply to live consistently, obeying the principles from Scripture we know to be true.

Daniel Had Undeterred Persistence and Faith

Although Nebuchadnezzar's top aide Ashpenaz empathized with Daniel's situation and request, as commander of the officials he was not immediately willing to risk his life and position to help Daniel and his friends (Daniel 1:10). In response, Daniel exhibited the kind of persistence and faith that is often necessary when a believer seeks a legitimate exemption from an official policy. Undeterred and believing he'd eventually receive the answer he wanted, Daniel diplomatically sought an alternate solution for his problem. The prophet and statesman simply appealed to a lower-ranking official who was more likely to grant the dietary request. Apparently, because he did not report directly to the king, that man was not afraid of Nebuchadnezzar as Ashpenaz was.

Daniel believed God was supporting his righteous convictions and would vindicate them. Therefore he exercised his faith and proposed a test to the other official: "Please test your servants for ten days, and let them give us vegetables to eat and water to drink. Then let our appearance be examined before you, and the appearance of the young men who eat the portion of the king's delicacies; and as you see fit, so deal with your servants" (Daniel 1:12–13). Daniel's message to the Babylonian officials was essentially this: "I'll put my faith to the test, and God will honor my uncompromising spirit."

The positive, scriptural characteristics that Daniel displayed when petitioning the Babylonian royal court paid off at the end of Daniel 1. Ashpenaz's assistant agreed to Daniel's ten-day test and the subsequent evaluation (1:14–16). By God's grace, the official recognized the benefits of Daniel's diet and allowed his friends and him to eat their diet rather than forcing them to consume Nebuchadnezzar's non-kosher cuisine.

Daniel's attitude, which comes through clearly from the entire account of Daniel 1, was crucial in his acquitting himself honorably in the midst of some challenging circumstances. His convictions were firm and settled, and his faith was untarnished and focused on God's will. The Lord honored that sincere and steadfast approach. He spared Daniel and his companions from reacting in the extreme. They did not passively cave in to a pagan government's unscriptural demands, nor did they respond in the opposite fashion and blindly resist what the Babylonians requested concerning diet.

Daniel's steady and godly performance in the arena of politics and government is an amazing testimony to the truth that God's sovereignty works in mysterious yet perfect harmony with man's responsibility. From a human perspective, Daniel was successful because he remained committed to the highest principles that were also right. From a divine perspective, everything worked out simply because God was in complete control of every detail. That profound, biblical truth also applies to us as we live for Christ before our neighbors and in the view of our leaders who rightly exercise certain authority over us.

Chapter 8

Paul's Example before Worldly Authorities

*His [Paul's] teachings and exemplary actions have relevance
to every aspect of the believer's life, so time and again
I'm compelled to uphold the great apostle as a role model for us.*

Chapter 8

Paul's Example before Worldly Authorities

The apostle Paul was a truly extraordinary figure, and not just in the New Testament or first-century history. He is arguably one of the five or ten greatest persons in world history, secular or sacred. Undoubtedly, except for our Lord Himself, he was the most influential and effective proponent of Christianity and the expansion of the church that the world has ever known.

With such an overwhelmingly prominent position in the annals of redemptive history, in most of my books I find it nearly impossible to exclude significant reference to the person and work of Paul. His teachings and exemplary actions have relevance to every aspect of the believer's life, so time and again I'm compelled to uphold the great apostle as a role model for us (see, for example, chapter 3, *The Power of Suffering* [Wheaton, Ill.: Victor, 1995]; chapter 6, *The Power of Integrity* [Wheaton, Ill.: Crossway, 1997]; chapter 10, *In the Footsteps of Faith* [Wheaton, Ill.: Crossway, 1998]). And this volume on the Christian's proper, biblically balanced responsibility toward politics and government is no exception.

The apostle Paul indeed was a model citizen and a knowledgeable one. The fact that he was officially a citizen of the Roman Empire was itself a great privilege in that time and culture. Roman citizenship carried with it certain significant benefits: the right to a fair hearing, exemption from scourging, the right to appeal to Caesar, and exemption from the poll tax. Paul was completely aware of those rights and privileges, and he knew how to appropriately take advantage of them in relating to the higher authorities. Robert Picirilli is correct when he writes,

> We understand Paul much better, then, if we remember that he was a citizen, born to a citizen, of the Roman Empire. His outlook and attitudes toward the world could not possibly have been unaffected by that relationship. He had a sense of identity with a heterogeneous world community, of being part of a united and far-flung empire, and of enjoying a certain standing in the established political structure.[1]

In this chapter we'll see not only how Paul recognized his role as a Christian and a Roman citizen before the governing officials but first of all how ideally he conducted himself under the scrutiny of the Jewish religious authorities as a Pharisee-turned-Christian. Much of the final fourth of the Book of Acts contains compelling material for such a study, but I think two accounts are sufficient to depict Paul's excellent example of relating in a godly fashion to worldly authority.

Paul was a prisoner of the Romans in the final chapters of Acts. His faithful, diligent, and tireless ministry efforts generated much hatred and opposition from the enemies of the gospel. Not long after his dramatic conversion, Paul "increased all the more in strength, and confounded the Jews who dwelt in Damascus, proving that this Jesus is the Christ" (Acts 9:22). That was a startling turnaround for one who had so recently persecuted the church (verse 21), and it so infuriated the Jews that they "plotted to kill him" (verse 23). However, Paul found out about the scheme and escaped with the help of other disciples (verses 24–25).

That early episode established a pattern for the rest of Paul's ministry. He faced animosity, resistance, and vigorous persecution nearly everywhere he ministered. Much to the apostle's profound grief (Romans 9:1–3), most of that opposition came from unbelieving Jews.

Near the end of his third missionary journey, those enemies of his preaching had Paul arrested in Jerusalem on trumped-up charges (Acts 21:27–33). That began a lengthy sequence in which he was constantly in custody and forced repeatedly to defend himself against the various false accusations. First, Paul testified on his own behalf from the steps of Fort Antonia (21:37–22:21), right after Roman soldiers had saved him from the angry temple mob. Then, when Claudius Lysias, the Roman commander in Jerusalem, could not use the scourging method of examination (because of Paul's Roman citizenship) to perhaps determine the apostle's precise crime, Paul had to face the Jewish Sanhedrin (22:30–23:11).

PAUL BEFORE THE SANHEDRIN

Throughout history, students of the New Testament have wondered how Lysias, a Gentile, had the authority to call a meeting of the Sanhedrin. But his was not a request for an official convening of the Jewish council. He was simply turning to the highest Jewish religious court for a clarification of the issues in dispute between Paul and the Jews. Furthermore, Lysias would not have turned a Roman citizen over for an actual trial when exact charges against the person were not yet established. In addition, the normal earmarks of an actual trial—formal charges brought, witnesses lined up to testify against Paul—were not present in this instance. Besides all that, it's likely that this informal convocation of the Sanhedrin occurred somewhere outside of Fort Antonia rather than in the usual meeting place on the temple grounds.

The Sanhedrin was the Jewish religious ruling body in Roman-occupied Israel. The council had final authority in matters concerning Jewish law, but it possessed only limited authority in civil matters. Roman governors (such as Pontius Pilate and Porcius Festus) and Roman-appointed leaders (the Herods) exercised the real political clout in Israel during Paul's time.

Out of the three main groups that made up the Sanhedrin (the high priests, the elders, and the scribes), two major religious factions dominated: the Sadducees and the Pharisees (see Acts 23:6). The council employed its own police force (see Acts 5:24–26) and sometimes administered punishment to those who violated Jewish law (Acts 5:40). However, Sanhedrin leaders could not carry out capital punishment

(John 18:31) unless the guilty individual had desecrated the temple.

Paul, as a one-time fanatic Pharisee, was aware of that basic background and was intelligently prepared to deal with the Sanhedrin in the following three phases of interaction.

Paul Confronts the Issues

The apostle Paul approached his session before the Sanhedrin with proper confidence and determination. Acts 23:1 describes it this way: "Then Paul, looking earnestly at the council, said, 'Men and brethren, I have lived in all good conscience before God until this day.'" His earnest look toward the Sanhedrin members was indicative of his conscious integrity. He knew that whatever way one viewed his situation—legally, morally, ethically, or religiously—he had done nothing wrong. Because of that, he had complete assurance that God was with him; therefore he did not have to cower in fear or guilt before the religious authorities.

Paul's bold assertion of a good conscience undoubtedly placed the Sanhedrin on the defensive. But such a statement was simply consistent with the apostle's original and ongoing Christian motivation to please and obey God (see Acts 24:16; Galatians 1:14; Philippians 3:6). He was merely trying to show members of the Sanhedrin right at the outset that by opposing him they were actually opposing God.

Paul was not saying all his words and actions had always been right. A good conscience is not the supreme factor in determining whether or not our actions toward authority are right or wrong (Paul's conscience once permitted him to oppose Christ). But in this situation Paul could rightly declare that he felt no guilt, in spite of the Sanhedrin's accusations. That's because his conscience was fully informed by Scripture and God's revelation.

He could accurately evaluate the circumstances before him and present an honorable testimony in front of the hostile religious leaders. Such discernment and righteous behavior will also be true of us, if our consciences are informed by the standards of God's Word (see 1 Corinthians 2:14–15; 4:4). Therefore we ought to sense, as those who want to conduct ourselves well before worldly authorities, the importance of faithfully reading, studying, and applying the Scripture.

The Leaders React to Paul's Claim

Paul's truthful, straightforward, and fair-minded defense of his position provoked an immediate backlash from the Sanhedrin's leadership. Consistent with his corrupt, brutal character, Ananias, the high priest, ordered those standing beside Paul to strike him (Acts 23:2). The blow was more than just a small slap to the face. Instead, it was similar to the kind of treatment the soldiers gave Jesus during His trial (see Matthew 27:30).

The beleaguered apostle quickly and angrily replied to Ananias's disgracefully illegal action: "God will strike you, you whitewashed wall! For you sit to judge me according to the law, and do you command me to be struck contrary to the law?" (Acts 23:3). On one hand, we can accept Paul's outburst as part of his indignation at the high priest's flouting of the law. (Paul was not really that concerned, as we might be, with the pain inflicted by the blow itself.) But on the other, we have to wonder why the apostle's harsh reply does not line up with admonitions elsewhere in the New Testament (for example, "Being reviled, we bless; being persecuted, we endure" [1 Corinthians 4:12]; or "when He was reviled, did not revile in return; when He suffered, He did not threaten" [1 Peter 2:23; see John 18:23]).

The answer is simple. Paul, although one of the godliest men who ever lived, was still a sinner. He battled with indwelling sin probably more diligently than most people (Romans 7:14–25.). But in this instance his flesh prevailed and he was not a good example of how one should show respect for authority.

Those standing beside Paul realized instantly that he was wrong, and they reprimanded him in very strong terms, "Do you *revile* God's high priest?" (Acts 23:4, emphasis added). Their choice of the Greek word translated "revile" shows they believed Paul's fierce language was not simply part of his legal strategy but a sinful expression of anger and disrespect. (Wherever else in the New Testament a form of this word *revile* appears, it is in a negative context, describing sinful behavior that should not characterize believers.)

However, the next verse proves the quality of Paul's character and provides us with an excellent example of how Christians ought to remedy their bad behavior and conduct themselves with humility before even the most hostile authority figures. Paul knew the principle that, even though he was evil and a disgrace to his office, Ananias was still owed respect rather than insult, simply because he occupied the divinely ordained leadership position of high priest (see Deuteronomy 17:8–12). Therefore the apostle humbly acknowledged his sin, "I did not know, brethren, that he was the high priest; for it is written, 'You shall not speak evil of a ruler of your people'" (Acts 23:5).

Paul responded in a manner befitting a mature believer. He didn't merely make an excuse for what he said, but he readily conceded that he had violated the command against slandering a ruler (Exodus 22:28). To show his respect for and submission to the authority of the Word, Paul even quoted that verse. By following his example and humbly taking responsibility for our words and actions, we can demonstrate that we care about our public testimony before those in authority. It's just one more way we can have an impact on our community as godly citizens.

Paul's Boldness Disrupts the Meeting

In the wake of such a sharp conflict with Ananias, Paul knew for sure the Sanhedrin would not grant him a fair hearing. Therefore, he was willing to risk further repercussions and forthrightly declare his position with the hope that at least one of the factions of the council would support him. "But when Paul perceived that one part were Sadducees and the other Pharisees, he cried out in the council, 'Men and brethren, I am a Pharisee, the son of a Pharisee; concerning the hope and resurrection of the dead I am being judged!' And when he had said this, a dissension arose between the Pharisees and the Sadducees; and the assembly was divided" (Acts 23:6–7).

As we mentioned earlier, the opposing factions of the Pharisees and Sadducees dominated the Sanhedrin. Paul, who in a certain sense considered himself still to be a Pharisee, appealed to them for support. The Pharisees believed in resurrection and the afterlife, whereas the Sadducees did not. So Paul's beliefs were more compatible with those of the Pharisees than with those of the Sadducees. The apostle undoubtedly knew that his appeal to the Pharisees would throw the hearing into disorder, and that's exactly what occurred (Acts 23:9).

But Paul persevered as one who understood his rights as a citizen and one who was willing to put his convictions on the line to achieve some measure of justice. And the Lord rewarded Paul's perseverance when Lysias, the secular official who referred him to the Sanhedrin in the first place, providentially intervened again: "Now when there arose a great dissension, the commander, fearing lest Paul might be pulled to pieces by them, commanded the soldiers to go down and take him by force from among them, and bring him into the barracks" (Acts 23:10). Lysias could see that Paul's situation was deteriorating from gross injustice to something perhaps far worse (death), and that his own frustration as a Roman official seeking to discover Paul's "crime" was only going to be further aggravated by the case's lack of resolution. Once again the Roman government worked to assist Paul in a crisis.

PAUL BEFORE PORCIUS FESTUS

In the aftermath of Paul's abortive appearance before the Sanhedrin, God providentially thrust on the apostle other opportunities to be the model of a godly citizen before worldly authorities. One of those notable occasions was his appearance before the Roman governor Porcius Festus—the final attempt in Judea for the Romans to resolve the Jews' accusations against Paul.

The authorities compelled the apostle to appear before Festus thanks to the previous governor Felix's inability and unwillingness to pass final sentence on Paul's case. After

Lysias sent Paul to Caesarea to extricate him from the Jews' murderous plot, he stood trial before Felix (Acts 23:12–35). None of the charges held up, but Felix, fearing the Jews and hoping for bribe money from Paul, issued no final acquittal but held the apostle in prison for another two years (Acts 24).

When Emperor Nero recalled the disgraced Felix after hearing of the governor's mishandling of a riot in Caesarea, the emperor soon sent Festus to be the new governor in Judea. Little is known of Festus' rule as governor, but historical references indicate he was a much more competent and decisive leader than Felix.

So Paul received another chance to present his case before a secular ruler, but this time before the tribunal of one who was determined to end the procrastination and settle the case concerning him.

An Old Plot Is Thwarted Again

When Festus arrived in Judea to begin his duties as governor, he inherited the political problems left by Felix's heavy-handed rule. His harsh and insensitive administration had alienated the Jews, and now they were suspicious and cynical toward Festus as well.

Festus also inherited Felix's most celebrated political and religious prisoner, the apostle Paul, who had been in prison and out of circulation for two years. Early in Festus' administration some of the Jewish leaders revived the charges against Paul in hopes of exploiting the new governor's inexperience and once and for all getting a conviction against the apostle before his case was summarily dismissed and he was released.

The Jews' request seemed legitimate and fair enough, as

Acts 25:2–3 reports it: "And they petitioned [Festus], asking a favor against [Paul], that he would summon him to Jerusalem." But their petition really involved an ulterior motive. They had no actual intention of ever allowing Paul to have another trial in Jerusalem; instead, they would kill him along the way to the city (verse 3). In reality, the Sanhedrin was reviving the old assassination plot that Lysias had thwarted two years earlier.

But providentially, the Jews could not dupe Festus into cooperating with their scheme. "But Festus answered that Paul should be kept at Caesarea, and that he himself was going there shortly. 'Therefore,' he said, 'let those who have authority among you go down with me and accuse this man, to see if there is any fault in him'" (Acts 25:4–5). In Festus' view, the proper location for Paul, a Roman citizen, to be tried was at the Roman city of Caesarea, which in Judea was like a county seat or provincial capital is today. Thus, in the midst of Festus' lack of experience as governor and lack of knowledge about Paul, combined with a desire to smooth out hard feelings between the Romans and Jews, God used him to preserve Paul's life.

Charges Are Renewed but Not Substantiated

Festus wasted little time before traveling to Caesarea and beginning a new trial—this time an official Roman one—for Paul. Once the apostle was again standing before the seat of justice, the contingent of Jews from Jerusalem swarmed around him like starving predators ready to rip apart their prey (see 25:6–7). But they were weak and ineffective predators who were unable to finish their task. The "many serious complaints" they brought against Paul actually consisted of the same mixed bag of charges (sedition, sectarianism, and sacrilege; see Acts 24:5–6) that the Jewish leaders could not prove two years earlier. They still had no credible witnesses, no solid evidence, and therefore no valid case against Paul.

The inability of his Jewish opponents to make any of their accusations stick emphasizes that Paul and other early Christians were good citizens (see Acts 18:12–28; 19:37). In spite of the frequent false allegations that the followers of Christ were nothing more than a sect of political revolutionaries, they were stellar examples of innocent, law-abiding subjects—a status all believers today should strive for. When Rome eventually persecuted and killed many in the early church, it was not because Christians were revolutionaries but because they refused to worship the emperor.

Since there was no evidence against him, it was rather easy for Paul to refute point by point the spurious charges: "He answered for himself, 'Neither against the law of the Jews [sectarianism], nor against the temple [sacrilege], nor against Caesar [sedition] have I offended in anything at all'" (Acts 25:8).

Paul's innocence placed a dilemma on Festus' shoulders—the same one that had so hamstrung Felix. Festus knew the facts of the case dictated Paul's release. But he also realized that to do so would antagonize the Jewish leaders and likely ruin any chance for him to peacefully coexist with them and have a trouble-free administration.

Unlike Felix (Acts 24:22–25), however, Festus sought a way out of the dilemma and proposed a compromise: "But Festus, wanting to do the Jews a favor, answered Paul and said, 'Are you willing to go up to Jerusalem and there be judged before me concerning these things?'" (25:9). The inexperienced governor no doubt considered his offer a reasonable compromise—it gave the Jews an opportunity to finally have Paul's trial in Jerusalem, and it reassured Paul that his Roman rights would be protected.

However, the apostle Paul, the consummate citizen of both the spiritual and civil realms (the onetime "Pharisee of the Pharisees," now the leading servant of Christ, and always a knowledgeable Roman subject), immediately understood that such a "compromise" in effect would give the Jews just what they wanted. They would simply dust off their ambush plans one more time and kill Paul on the way back to Jerusalem. If they had their way, no further trial for Paul would even take place.

Paul therefore, confident in his course of action, rejected Festus' proposal, reminded the governor of his (Paul's) Roman legal rights, again proclaimed his innocence, and stated that his motives were honorable. Here's how Luke, the physician and historian, recorded Paul's defense: "I stand at Caesar's judgment seat, where I ought to be judged. To the Jews I have done no wrong, as you very well know. For if I am an offender, or have committed anything deserving of death, I do not object to dying; but if there is nothing in these things of which these men accuse me, no one can deliver me to them" (Acts 25:10–11).

Paul was so confident that his position was right that he was willing to suffer the consequences if his firm appeal for justice was undercut or later denied. As a good Roman citizen, he was not attempting to evade justice but simply insisting that justice be granted him in a Roman courtroom.

The Jews' empty case against him meant there was no obligation for him to allow them to resolve his difficult situation.

Besides, even if he did survive a journey back to Jerusalem, the Jews would almost certainly make sure he lost his trial and consequently his life. The apostle really had nothing to lose, so he chose a bold next step, one that was perfectly legal.

Paul Appeals to Caesar

Because Paul knew that Festus' compromise proposal to the Jews effectively removed any chance that the apostle would receive a fair trial in Jerusalem, Paul exercised his right as a Roman citizen and appealed to the emperor. If such an appeal were honored, the governor would transfer Paul's case into the direct jurisdiction of Caesar.

Paul's dramatic plea allowed Festus to resolve his dilemma. After a brief conference with his advisors, the governor accepted Paul's appeal: "You have appealed to Caesar? To Caesar you shall go!" (Acts 25:12). The Lord was faithful to His promise (Acts 23:11), and Paul was finally going to Rome.

LESSONS FROM PAUL

Several important lessons emerge for us from the apostle Paul's ordeals before the official bench of worldly authority. I believe they apply to us not only in the area of godly citizenship and respect for those who rule over us, but also in the realm of our general Christian walk and testimony before others.

First of all, what happened to Paul in his confrontations with worldly authorities clearly reveals the triumph of God's sovereignty over human affairs (see Genesis 45:7–8; Daniel

4:17; Luke 22:53; John 7:30; 19:10–11; Acts 2:23). That sovereignty was displayed as Claudius Lysias rescued Paul from the frenzied hatred and murderous designs of the Sanhedrin. Likewise, we saw the providence of God working through the person of Porcius Festus as he spared Paul the need to return to Jerusalem and have a final hearing so close to all his Jewish enemies. But perhaps the ultimate way God's sovereignty controlled events in Paul's relationship to worldly authorities and government was the fact that the Lord arranged for him to be born a Roman citizen in Tarsus. And the apostle knew how to utilize his rights and privileges as a citizen of Rome to their full legal and ethical extent. And he did so in a God-honoring fashion that held high his Christian testimony—and so should we in dealing with the authorities God has placed us under.

Second, Paul used his circumstances as an opportunity to witness, or at least speak a word that honored God or edified others (Acts 23:1, 6; 25:8; see 22:1–21; 24:10–21). Giving a complete gospel presentation was not his main goal every time he testified at a civil hearing, but he did not remain silent when it was appropriate to enhance his defense with a word about the reason for the hope within his heart (see 1 Peter 3:15).

Third, Paul always endeavored to maintain the proper attitude. Even when he momentarily lost his composure and reacted sinfully, he was quick to acknowledge his sin and bad judgment and set things right (Acts 23:3–5). His general attitude was one of love and submission, aware of his God-given citizenship rights but willing to obey and follow official procedures that might temporarily restrict those rights (see, for example, 22:27–30; 26:32).

Finally, all of Paul's words and actions before various

worldly authorities summarize for us in a practical way and remind us again of the theme of this volume, that God expects the believer to relate properly to governmental authority. Paul willingly respected and obeyed even the most unworthy authorities, and he practiced what he taught in Romans 13:1–5. We've already studied in detail what the apostle said there about government and the Christian, but I think it's helpful to review those words as we seek to make them part of our lives:

> Let every soul be subject to the governing authorities. For there is no authority except from God, and the authorities that exist are appointed by God. Therefore whoever resists the authority resists the ordinance of God, and those who resist will bring judgment on themselves. For rulers are not a terror to good works, but to evil. Do you want to be unafraid of the authority? Do what is good, and you will have praise from the same. For he is God's minister to you for good. But if you do evil, be afraid; for he does not bear the sword in vain; for he is God's minister, an avenger to execute wrath on him who practices evil. Therefore you must be subject, not only because of wrath but also for conscience' sake.

Chapter 9

How to Live in a Pagan Culture

With society sliding headlong into greater and greater evil, debauchery, violence, and corruption, and seemingly populated outside the church by no one but "modern barbarians," the temptation is strong for believers to jump into the cultural fray as self-righteous social/political reformers and condescending moralizers.

Chapter 9

How to Live in a Pagan Culture

A quarter century ago the late apologist and Christian thinker Francis Schaeffer asked the question, "How should we then live?" in his landmark book of the same title. The relevance of that question has not changed. If anything, it has only become more urgent for believers at the dawn of a new century and millennium. With society sliding headlong into greater and greater evil, debauchery, violence, and corruption, and seemingly populated outside the church by no one but "modern barbarians," the temptation is strong for believers to jump into the cultural fray as self-righteous social/political reformers and condescending moralizers. All the while those self-styled Christian activists forget or ignore their true mission in the world and completely miss the answer to our lead question—an answer that God's Word spells out quite clearly.

As noble as the desire to reform society may be, and as stirring as the emotions sometimes are when we're involved in a political cause we really believe is right, those activities are not to be the Christian's chief priorities. As we have seen in the previous chapters of this volume, God does not call the church to influence the culture by promoting legislation and court rulings that advance a scriptural point of view. Nor does He condone any type of radical activism that would avoid tax obligations, disobey or seek removal of government officials we don't agree with, or spend an inordinate amount of time campaigning for a so-called Christian slate of candidates.

The church will really change society for the better only when individual believers make their chief concern their own spiritual maturity, which means living in a way that honors God's commands and glorifies His name. Such a concern inherently includes a firm grasp on Scripture and an understanding that its primary mandate to us is to know Christ and proclaim His gospel. A godly attitude coupled with godly living makes the saving message of the gospel credible to the unsaved. If we claim to be saved but still convey proud, unloving attitudes toward the lost, our preaching and teaching—no matter how doctrinally orthodox or politically savvy and persuasive—will be ignored or rejected.

The New Testament elucidates how we ought to embrace and live out our primary mission in a pagan society. One such passage is Titus 3:1–8. It's the beginning of the final chapter of an epistle in which the apostle Paul is obviously concerned about the divine command to advance God's kingdom. He simply followed his Lord's example and did not expend time and energy admonishing believers on how to reform pagan culture's idolatrous, immoral, and corrupt practices. The apostle also did not call for believers to exercise civil disobedience to protest the Roman Empire's unjust laws or cruel punishments. Instead, his appeal was for Christians to proclaim the gospel and live lives that would give clear evidence to its transforming power. And so it was in his instructions to Titus.

In Titus 3:1–8 Paul uses a call to remembrance to exhort us to be faithful to our Christian duties in a sinful world. He begins verse 1 with "remind," the translation of a Greek imperative of command that governs all the admonitions in the passage. The word is also in the present tense, which further implies that believers ought to continually remember the truths that motivate them in loving the unsaved. There are four such areas of spiritual truth that merit regular reminding: our Christian duties, our unsaved condition, our salvation, and our mission.

REMEMBERING OUR CHRISTIAN DUTIES

Paul, under the inspiration of the Holy Spirit, begins his call to remembrance by listing seven duties that always apply to Christians and define our obligation to secular society: "Remind them to be subject to rulers and authorities, to obey, to be ready for every good work, to speak evil of no one, to be peaceable, gentle, showing all humility to all men" (Titus 3:1–2).

Consistently demonstrating willing obedience for human authority shows unbelievers that, even though the things of this life are not our primary focus, we still have respect for government and loving concern for other citizens. As Christians, our true citizenship is in heaven (Philippians 3:20), and our main focus must be on holy living and on reaching the lost, because our Lord Himself came "to seek and to save that which was lost" (Luke 19:10). When we do live as God wants us to in an unbelieving culture, that in itself can make the attitude of the lost more receptive to God (1 Peter 2:12).

Obey Government and All Authority

The first two duties—submission to government and obedience to all human authority—I've combined under one heading because they are so closely related. And in keeping with the first eight chapters of this volume, they are just one more reminder that Christians have certain requirements of attitude and conduct in relation to our secular leaders. These reminders reiterate our theme that believers are not exempt from following civil laws and directives unless such orders contradict the Word and will of God (see Acts 4:18–20; 5:40–42). This twofold prompting also gives us the scriptural premise from which all our other public actions ought to flow.

Be Prepared for Good Works

Our third major duty toward society is to have a readiness "for every good work." Here the apostle Paul is not referring to some minimal, reluctant adherence to doing what we already know is right, but to a sincere willingness and heart preparation to do good works to everyone, as we have the opportunity. No matter how antagonistic the people around us may be, we are to be kind servants to them when their lives intersect with ours. "Therefore, as we have opportunity, let us do good to all, especially to those who are of the household of faith" (Galatians 6:10).

God wants us recognized for what we might call "consistent and aggressive goodness"—good deeds done out of love for the Lord and love for other people.

Do Not Malign Anyone

Next, we have the scriptural duty of not maligning anyone, not even those unbelievers who are most antagonistic toward biblical standards. Titus 3:2 begins with Paul's command "to speak evil of no one," and refers to cursing, slandering, and treating with contempt. In fact the Greek term rendered "speak evil of" is the one from which we derive the English *blasphemy.* We can never use such speech with a righteous motive.

It is sad that many believers today speak scornfully of politicians and other public figures. When they do that, they actually manifest a basic disregard of their responsibility toward authority and hinder God's redemptive plan. In another of Paul's pastoral letters, he urges us to pray for everyone's salvation, even for that of those who occupy official positions of authority (1 Timothy 2:1–4).

Be Peaceful and Gentle to Everyone

Paul goes on in Titus 3:2 to mention two more Christian duties. First, he reminds us that we must be friendly and peaceful toward the lost, not belligerent and quarrelsome. In the ungodly, postmodern world we live in, it's easy to condemn those who contribute to the culture's demise and write them off as corrupt sinners who will never change. If God's love for the world was so broad and intense that His Son died for a multitude of sinners (John 3:16), how can we who have received that redeeming grace be harsh and unloving toward those who have not yet received it? Until God is pleased to save an individual, he or she is going to behave like an unbeliever, and it is wrong for us, meanwhile, to treat him contemptuously for acting according to his nature. On the contrary, Romans 12:18 encourages us, "If it is possible, as much as depends on you, live peaceably with all men."

Secondly, Paul reminds us that we must be "gentle," a word in the Greek that means being fair, moderate, and forbearing toward others. Some have translated this term "sweet reasonableness," a definition denoting an attitude that does not hold grudges but gives others the benefit of the doubt.

Be Considerate of Others

The final duty in the apostle Paul's list of reminders to believers is that they should be "showing all humility to all men" (Titus 3:2). The word rendered "humility," probably more clearly translated "consideration" (as in the NASB), always has a New Testament meaning of genuine concern for others.

Scripture clearly describes Jesus as the One supremely characterized by humility, or consideration for everyone—the same trait that should identify His followers. First, the Greek translation of Zechariah 9:9 portrays Him that way: "He is just and having salvation, lowly and riding on a donkey, a colt, the foal of a donkey" (see also Matthew 21:5). Then Jesus used the word to depict Himself when He told His followers, "Take My yoke upon you and learn from Me, for I am *gentle* and lowly in heart, and you will find rest for your souls" (Matthew 11:29, emphasis added).

All our dealings with unbelievers should display this kind of attitude, as the apostle Peter wrote, "Sanctify the Lord God in your hearts, and always be ready to give a defense to everyone who asks you a reason for the hope that is in you, with meekness and fear" (1 Peter 3:15).

Therefore it is understandable that *consideration* is one aspect of the fruit of the Spirit (translated again as "gentleness" in Galatians 5:23), and that the adjective form is a beatitude ("meek," Matthew 5:5; see also Colossians 3:12).

Sincere, heartfelt "humility [consideration, meekness, gentleness] to all men" is foundational for our Christian walk in a pagan society. Our duty as we relate to an increasingly secular and ungodly culture is not to lobby for certain rights, the implementation of a Christian agenda, or the reformation of the government. Rather, God would have us continually to remember Paul's instructions to Titus and live them out as we seek to demonstrate His power and grace that can regenerate sinners. Changing people's hearts one individual at a time is the only way to bring meaningful, lasting change to our communities and nations.

REMEMBERING OUR UNSAVED CONDITION

Whenever we are tempted to self-righteously criticize and disparage unbelieving political leaders, journalists, educators, and entertainers, and whenever we find it easy to make angry, sarcastic attacks against the increasingly ungodly viewpoints and practices of society, we need to remind ourselves as Paul did Christians in Titus 3:3, "For we ourselves were also once foolish, disobedient, deceived, serving various lusts and pleasures, living in malice and envy, hateful and hating one another."

Before we were Christians, we did not all practice or promote the grossest, most heinous sins, but we all were depraved in our natures and at enmity with God (Romans 5:10; Ephesians 2:3; Colossians 1:21). That was true no matter how externally moral, respectable, religiously "orthodox," or politically conservative we may have been.

As we become more mature in the faith and more devoted to the truths of God's Word, it is increasingly distressing and infuriating to witness the accelerating demise of contemporary culture. First we face all around us a social and political environment that endorses "political correctness," New Age philosophy, "abortion rights," and the excesses of modern psychotherapy (a preoccupation with self-esteem, considering everyone who has problems "a victim," viewing sin as merely an addiction, etc.). Added to that, there is the increased tolerance of sexual promiscuity and marital infidelity, homosexuality as just an "alternate lifestyle," and pornography as simply another "freedom of expression." And all of those attitudes seem to be encouraged by film and television producers who want to include ever more sexually explicit and violently graphic content in their works. And on top of it all, we read about and hear of immorality, dishonesty, and corruption at the highest political levels. Unquestionably, such trends are unbiblical and sinful, destructive to individuals, and counter-productive to society as a whole.

But to some degree, with certain variations, such a situation has been true since the Fall and will be so until Christ returns. That reality should remind us that ungodly opinions and actions are simply to be expected from unbelievers. The sad state of the world need not hinder us from presenting a godly testimony to people who so desperately need to see the validity of the gospel lived out and proclaimed to them. To sharpen our perspective and maintain our priorities, it is helpful to remember that we were once much like the unbelievers who so often irritate us. Let's define each expression on the list of sins in Titus 3:3 and remind ourselves that, but for God's grace, we would yet be engaged in some or all of those vices.

- "Foolish" means one who is ignorant and uninformed. They completely lack understanding about a particular subject. You might have had the most advanced educational background and a successful career, but until you by faith accepted the gospel and repented of your sins, you were utterly foolish in how you thought and lived.

- "Disobedient" means just what it indicates. Outside of Christ, all people were and are inherently unable and unwilling to submit to divinely instituted authority (see Jeremiah 17:9; Matthew 15:19–20). God uses human laws and regulations to maintain order and safety in society and to punish wrongdoing. But such ordinances by themselves are unable to transform human hearts and make men and women ultimately good.

- Third, Paul reminds us that while we were unsaved we were naturally "deceived." The word essentially means to be purposely led astray. It describes what Satan is doing to a greater and greater extent in the lives of sinners (Matthew 24:24; John 8:44; Revelation 12:9; see 2 Timothy 3:13).

- "Serving various lusts and pleasures" actually denotes an enslavement to sin in all its forms (see Romans 3:10–18; 6:19). Before salvation, we all not only willfully served sin but also did so slavishly because we had neither the desire nor the spiritual ability to do otherwise. "Lusts" are sinful desires and "pleasures" are sinful satisfactions. (The Greek word for "pleasures" gives us the English term *hedonism,* the voracious pursuit of self-satisfaction that's so typical of contemporary culture.)

- The apostle Paul goes on to remind us that before we knew Christ we were "living in malice and envy." As a normal, typical pattern of life, we were doing "malice," or practicing evil and exhibiting vicious personal character. "Envy" by definition means one will be dissatisfied with what he or she has and will always be craving more.

- Hate is a natural by-product of envy, but many other factors can also cause it. Sometimes people simply express it for no apparent reason. Hate loathes anyone or anything that stands in its way or displeases it. Those who are "hateful and hating" are rather soon alienated from everyone. Thus hate is perhaps the loneliest of sins.

The preceding sins, along with other iniquities, have made unbelievers spiritually insensitive to what God demands of them and what He desires in a righteous society. Hence, non-Christians have produced the kind of culture we have today. And although we detest the sinful, unbiblical aspects of society, we must remember that the same ungodly characteristics once defined our lives. Such awareness will keep us humble and prevent us from putting down sinners simply because they rub us the wrong way by their values and lifestyles. Our unbelieving neighbors don't need merely to be set straight about their political and moral choices; they need soul-transforming salvation through Jesus Christ, just as you and I once did.

REMEMBERING OUR SALVATION

The apostle Paul also recognized in his sequence of reminders to believers that it is vitally important that they remember their current status as saved individuals. He writes that crucial reminder in the next portion of Titus 3, one long sentence that encompasses all the glorious truths and wonderful facets of God's sovereign salvation:

> But when the kindness and the love of God our Savior toward man appeared, not by works of righteousness which we have done, but according to His mercy He saved us, through the washing of regeneration and renewing of the Holy Spirit, whom He poured out on us abundantly through Jesus Christ our Savior, that having been justified by His grace we should become heirs according to the hope of eternal life. (verses 4–7)

God's Overwhelming Kindness

The first aspect of salvation Paul would have us remember is that our redemption issued wholly from God's kindness. It was only because of His loving and gracious concern for us that He rescued us from sin and drew us to Himself so that we would never be lost again. It is simply God's nature to be kind to His children: "But God, who is rich in mercy, because of His great love with which He loved us, even when we were dead in trespasses, made us alive together with Christ (by grace you have been saved), and raised us up together, and made us sit together in the heavenly places in Christ Jesus, that in the ages to come He might show the exceeding riches of His grace in His kindness toward us in Christ Jesus" (Ephesians 2:4–7). His sovereign kindness initiates repentance, the first step in our salvation (Romans 2:4; see also 11:22).

God's Undeserved Love for Mankind

Second, lest we act arrogantly toward unbelievers in society and look condescendingly toward their unscriptural lifestyles, we ought not to forget that God's uninfluenced and unearned love for humanity saved us. "Love . . . toward man" in Titus 3:4 is from the Greek compound noun that gives us the familiar English word *philanthropy.* The original expression means to deliver someone from pain, distress, or danger, and to do so in a way that is tangibly helpful, not just sentimentally emotional.

In verse 4, "love . . . toward man" and "kindness" are virtually synonymous in meaning and nuance. That ought to cause us to reflect further on the deeper *agape* love God had for the fallen world (John 3:16). And that ought to cause us to be constantly grateful for the life we have (Galatians 2:20) and the life others who will yet believe can have: "For God did not send His Son into the world to condemn the world, but that the world through Him might be saved" (John 3:17).

God's Mercy

The apostle Paul would also have us remember the profound

teaching of Titus 3:5: "Not by works of righteousness which we have done, but according to His mercy He saved us, through the washing of regeneration and renewing of the Holy Spirit." Being saved is the most precious and important reality that Christians can know and appreciate. Salvation has delivered us from the predicament of being spiritually dead, enslaved to the penalty of sin, living under God's wrath, and on our way to hell (see again John 3:16–17, along with verse 36). As a result, it has also granted us the privilege of being made "alive together with Christ" (Ephesians 2:5), of being "conveyed . . . into the kingdom of the Son of His love" (Colossians 1:13), of being able "to come to the knowledge of the truth" (1 Timothy 2:4), and of attaining "hope of eternal life" (Titus 1:2).

Titus 3:5 is a clear reminder that our salvation was not based on anything we were, had done, or ever could do (see also Ephesians 2:8–9). Instead, it derives from God's mercy, or from His outward display of pity that assumed we had a need and knew He had more than enough resources to meet it.

The Washing of Regeneration

When God mercifully saved us, He granted us the "washing of regeneration." That means He washed away our sins and all the spiritual decay and moral filth produced by our spiritual deadness. Elsewhere Paul explains that this cleansing occurred "with the washing of water by the word" (Ephesians 5:26; see also James 1:18; 1 Peter 1:23).

"Regeneration" in the original language contains the concept of being born again, born from above, or receiving new life. It's the same vital truth Jesus declared to Nicodemus in

John 3:5 and 7: "Most assuredly, I say to you, unless one is born of water and the Spirit, he cannot enter the kingdom of God. . . . Do not marvel that I said to you, 'You must be born again.'" The apostle John, in his first epistle, makes a number of additional references intended to give us reassurance about what it means to be born again (2:29; 3:9; 4:7; 5:1, 18).

The Holy Spirit's Renewing Work

Paul moves to the next logical phase of salvation, the result of regeneration, when he concludes Titus 3:5 by mentioning the "renewing of the Holy Spirit." That's a reminder of and reference to the new life that emerges from the new birth. The Spirit of God, working through the Word of God, enables us to have a new life in Christ. "If anyone is in Christ, he is a new creation; old things have passed away; behold, all things have become new" (2 Corinthians 5:17; see also Romans 8:2). That's the beginning of the Holy Spirit's work of sanctification in our lives as believers (see 2 Corinthians 3:18; 1 Peter 1:2), a reminder that ought to encourage us every day as we live in the midst of a decaying society and seek to have an impact on it.

And with His help we will have an impact on pagan culture and secular government because the Holy Spirit not only renewed us, but God also poured Him out on us abundantly. For that reason, the Lord "is able to do exceedingly abundantly above all that we ask or think, according to the power that works in us" (Ephesians 3:20; see also Acts 2:38–39).

A Foundation on Christ's Death

If anything should prevent us from feeling hostile toward the corrupters of contemporary society and keep us from wasting our time trying to bring about moral and political reform, it should be the reminder that all the wonderful benefits of salvation derive from Jesus Christ's atoning sacrifice on the cross. In 2 Timothy 1:9, Paul states in greater detail the basis of our salvation and implicitly what that calls us to: "[God] has saved us and called us with a holy calling, not according to our works, but according to His own purpose and grace which was given to us in Christ Jesus before time began" (see also Romans 4:2–8; Ephesians 2:8–10).

Paul cited his own experience as proof that salvation is based entirely and only on the gracious, merciful, substitutionary work of Christ, and to argue that believers must not get caught up in their *own* good works and religious credentials.

> If anyone else thinks he may have confidence in the flesh, I more so: circumcised the eighth day, of the stock of Israel, of the tribe of Benjamin, a Hebrew of the Hebrews; concerning the law, a Pharisee; concerning zeal, persecuting the church; concerning the righteousness which is in the law, blameless. But what things were gain to me, these I have counted loss for Christ. Yet indeed I also count all things loss for the excellence of the knowledge of Christ Jesus my Lord, for whom I have suffered the loss of all things, and count them as rubbish, that I may gain Christ and be found in Him, not having my own righteousness, which is from the law, but that which is through faith

in Christ, the righteousness which is from God by faith. (Philippians 3:4–9)

Our position as people who are saved by the sovereign grace of God provides us with a great hope for the future that ought to daily motivate us and keep us focused on our real priorities. The apostle Paul reminds Titus and us that we have "become heirs according to the hope of eternal life" (Titus 3:7). He expands on this marvelous truth more fully in Romans, "The Spirit Himself bears witness with our spirit that we are children of God, and if children, then heirs-heirs of God and joint heirs with Christ, if indeed we suffer with Him, that we may also be glorified together" (8:16–17; see also 1 Peter 1:3–4).

All these reminders about our salvation culminate in one easy-to-remember, three-word summary: *He saved us!* And that directs us to Paul's fourth and final reminder concerning what believers are to be about while they are living as salt and light in this evil world.

REMEMBERING OUR MISSION

How can we live in a pagan society in a God-honoring manner, in such a way that we do not alienate the very people God wants us to reach with the gospel? We must remember to be engaged in good works, which Scripture says will result from our salvation. Paul summarizes the final reminder well in Titus 3:8: "This is a faithful saying, and these things I want you to affirm constantly, that those who have believed in God should be careful to maintain good works. These things are good and profitable to men." We simply need to understand and obey all the instructions the apostle, through the

Holy Spirit, gives us in the pastoral letters (and in all his New Testament letters) concerning what the body of Christ is and how it ought to function while still on earth.

If all that is true of you, you will recognize that it is not your primary calling to change your culture, to reform the outward moral behavior and professed political convictions of those around you, or to remake society superficially, according to some kind of "evangelical Christian blueprint." Instead, you will constantly remember that the Lord has called you to be His witness before the lost and condemned world in which you now live. Such a mission is far more "good and profitable to men" than any amount of social and political activism. Such endeavors may renovate people's outward lives, but they cannot transform their hearts and bring them to a saving relationship with Jesus Christ. That ultimate transformation will happen only as you and other faithful believers cheerfully perform your Christian duties (including submission to human authority), remember your previous lost condition and your current saved one, and then diligently "maintain good works"—works that are scripturally informed and empowered by the Holy Spirit to convert sinners and produce lasting spiritual fruit.

Appendix

—⊷◈⊶—

Citizenship in Heaven

**A SERMON DELIVERED ON SUNDAY EVENING,
OCTOBER 12, 1862**
*By Charles Haddon Spurgeon at The Metropolitan Tabernacle,
Newington (London, England)*

(Editor's note: The following sermon has been edited for vocabulary, style, and format to make it more accessible to the contemporary reader. The substance of Spurgeon's thought has not been altered. All Scripture quotations are now from the New King James Version.)

> For our citizenship is in heaven, from which we also eagerly wait for the Savior, the Lord Jesus Christ. (Philippians 3:20)

There can be no comparison between a soaring seraph and a crawling worm. Christian people ought so to live that it were idle to speak of a comparison between them and the people of the world. It should not be a comparison but a contrast. No scale of degrees should be possible;

the believer should be a direct and manifest contradiction to the unregenerate. The life of a saint should be altogether above and removed from the direction of the life of a sinner. We should compel our critics not to confess that moralists are good and Christians a little better, but while the world is darkness, we should manifestly be light. And while the world lies in the Wicked One, we should most evidently be of God and overcome the temptations of that Wicked One. Wide as the distance between the poles are life and death, light and darkness, health and disease, purity and sin, spiritual and carnal, divine and sensual. If we were what we profess to be, we should be as distinct a people in the midst of this world as a white race in a community of dark-skinned people. There should be no more difficulty in detecting the Christian from the worldly person than in discovering a sheep from a goat or a lamb from a wolf. Alas, the Church is so much adulterated that we have to lessen our glorying and cannot exalt her character as we would. "The precious sons of Zion, valuable as fine gold, how they are regarded as clay pots, the work of the hands of the potter!" (Lamentations 4:2).

O for the time when our citizenship will be in heaven and the shameful life of the man, whose god is his belly and whose end is destruction, will be rebuked by our unworldly, unselfish character. There should be as much difference between the worldly person and the Christian as between hell and heaven, between destruction and eternal life. As we hope at last that there will be a great gulf separating us from the doom of the impenitent, there should be here a deep and wide gulf between us and the ungodly. The purity of our character should be such that people must take knowledge of us that we are of another, superior race. God grant us more and more to be most clearly "a chosen generation, a royal priesthood, a holy nation, His own special people, that [we] may proclaim the praises of Him who called [us] out of darkness into His marvelous light" (1 Peter 2:9).

Brethren, tonight I exhort you to holiness—not by the precepts of the law, not by the thunderings from Sinai, not by the perils or punishments which might fall upon you if you are unholy but by the privileges to which you have been admitted. Gracious souls should only be urged by arguments from grace. Whips are for the backs of fools and not for heirs of heaven. By the honorable citizenship which has been bestowed upon you, I will beseech you to let your life be in heaven, and I will urge that most prevailing argument, that the Lord Jesus Christ is coming. Therefore we should be as people who watch for our Lord, diligently doing service unto Him, that when He comes he may say unto us, "Well done, good and faithful servants." I know that the grace which is in you will freely answer to such a plea.

Our text, I think, might be best translated as it is: "Our citizenship is in heaven." The French translation renders it, "As for us, our burgess-ship is in the heavens." Doddridge paraphrases it, "But we converse as citizens of heaven, considering ourselves as denizens of the New Jerusalem, and only strangers and pilgrims upon earth."

The first idea which is suggested by the verse under consideration is this: if our citizenship be in heaven, then **we are aliens here;** we are strangers and foreigners, pilgrims and sojourners on the earth, as all our ancestors were. In the words of Holy Scripture, "For here we have no continuing city, but we seek the one to come" (Hebrews 13:14). Let us illustrate our position. A certain young man is sent out by his father to trade on behalf of the family. He is sent to America, and he is just now living in New York. A very fortunate thing it is for him that his citizenship is in England; that, though he lives in America and trades there, yet he is an alien and does not belong to that afflicted nation; for he retains his citizenship with us on this side of the Atlantic. Yet there is a certain conduct which is due from him to the country which affords him shelter, and he must see to it that he does not fail to render it. Since we are aliens, we must remember to behave ourselves as aliens should and by no means come short in our duty. We are affected by the position of our temporary country.

A person trading in New York or Boston, though a citizen of the city of London, will find himself very much affected by the trade of the dis-United States [Editor's note: Americans were then in the midst of the Civil War]. When the merchants of his city suffer, he will find himself suffering with them. The fluctuations of their money market will affect his undertakings, and the stagnation of commerce will slacken his progress. But if prosperity should happily return, he will find that when the accounts of their merchants are getting wealthy, his will be that much better; and the happy development of trade will encourage his own ventures. He is not of the nation, and yet every trembling of the scale will affect him. He will prosper as that nation prospers, and he will suffer as that nation suffers—that is to say, not as a citizen but as a trader. And so we in this country find that, though we are strangers and foreigners on earth, yet we share all the inconveniences of the flesh. No exemption is granted to us from the common lot of humanity. We are born to trouble, even as others, and have tribulation like the rest. When famine comes, we hunger. When war rages, we are in danger, exposed to the same climate, bearing the same burning heat, or the same freezing cold. We know the whole array of suffering, even as the citizens of earth know them.

When God in mercy scatters liberally with both His hands the bounties of His providence, we take our share. Though we are aliens, yet we live upon the good of the land, and share the tender mercies of the God of providence. Hence we have to take some interest in it; and the good man, though he be a foreigner, will not live even a week in this foreign land without seeking to do good among the neighbors with whom he dwells. The good Samaritan sought not only the good of the Samaritan nation, but of the Jews. Though there was no sort of kinship among them (for the Samaritans were not, as we have often heard erroneously said, first cousins or relations to the Jews; not a drop of Jewish blood ever ran in the Samaritans' veins; they were strangers brought from Assyria; they had no relation to Abraham whatever), yet the good Samaritan, finding himself traveling between Jericho and Jerusalem, did good to the Jew since he was in Judea. The Lord charged His people by His servant Jeremiah, "Seek the peace of the city where I have caused you to be carried away captive, and pray to the LORD for it; for in its peace you will have peace" (Jeremiah 29:7). Since we are here, we must seek the good of this world. "Do not forget to do good and to share" (Hebrews 13:16). "Love your enemies, do good, and lend, hoping for nothing in return; and your reward will be great, and you will be sons of the Most High. For he is kind to the unthankful and evil" (Luke 6:35).

We must do our utmost while we are here to bring people to Christ, to win them from their evil ways, to bring them to eternal life, and to make them, with us, citizens of another and a better land. For, to tell the truth, we are here as recruiting sergeants for heaven, to give men the enlisting money, to bind upon them the blood red colors of the Savior's service, to win them to King Jesus, that, by and by, they may share His victories after having fought His battles.

Seeking the good of the country as aliens, we must also remember that it benefits aliens to keep themselves very quiet. What business have foreigners to plot against the government, or to intermeddle with the politics of a country in which they have no citizenship? An Englishman in New York had best be without a tongue just now; if he should criticize the courage of the generals, the accuracy of their dispatches, or the genius of the president, he might receive some harsh responses. He will be injudicious, indeed, if he cannot leave America to the Americans. So, in this land of ours, where you and I are strangers, we must be orderly sojourners, submitting ourselves constantly to those who are in authority, leading orderly and peaceable lives, and, according to the command of the Holy Spirit through the apostle, "honor all people. Love the brotherhood. Fear God. Honor the king" (1 Peter 2:17); "submit yourselves to every ordinance of man for the Lord's sake" (verse 13).

I cannot say that I delight in political Christians. I fear that party strife is a serious trial to believers, and I cannot reconcile our heavenly citizenship with the schemes of the campaign trail and the stress of the polling booth. You must follow your own judgment here, but for my part, I am a foreigner even in England, and as such I mean to act. We are simply passing through this earth, and should bless it in our transit, but never yoke ourselves to its affairs. An Englishman may happen to be in Spain. He wishes a thousand things were different from what they are, but he does not trouble himself much about them. Says he, "If I were a Spaniard, I would see what I could do to alter this government, but, being an Englishman, let the Spaniards see to their own matters. I will be back to my own country by and by, and the sooner the better." So with Christians here; they are content very much to let the worldly people deal with the worldly things of the earth. Their politics concern their own country; they do not care much about any other. As men they love liberty and are not willing to lose it even in the lower sense. But spiritually, their politics are spiritual, and as citizens they look to the interest of that divine republic to which they belong. And they wait for the time when, having patiently borne with the laws of the land of their exile, they will come under the more gracious rule of Him who reigns in glory, the King of kings and Lord of lords. "If it is possible, as much as depends on you, live peaceably with all men" (Romans 12:18). Serve your day and generation still, but do not build your soul's dwelling place here, for all this earth must be destroyed at the coming of the fiery day.

Again, let us remember that as aliens *we have privileges as well as duties.* The princes of evil cannot draft us into their regiments; we cannot be compelled to do Satan's work. The king of this world may make his vassals serve him, but he cannot conscript aliens into his service. He may order out his troops to this villainy or to that wicked service, but the child of God claims an immunity from all the commands of Satan. Let evil maxims bind the men who are slaves to them. We are free and not subject to the prince of the power of the air. I know that men of this world say we must keep up appearances; we must be respectable; we must do as others do; we must swim with the tide; we must move with the crowd; but not so the upright believer. "No," says he, "do not expect me to fall in with your ways and customs; I am in Rome, but I will not do as Rome does. I will let you see that I am an alien, and that I have rights as an alien, even here in this foreign land. I am not to be bound to fight your battles, nor march at the sound of your drums."

Brethren, we are soldiers of Christ. We are enlisted in *His* army, and as aliens here, we are not to be constrained into the army of evil. Let lords and lands have what masters they will, let us be free, for Christ is our Master still. The seventy thousand, whom God has reserved, will not bow the knee to Baal. Let it be known unto you, O world, that we will not serve your gods, nor worship the image you have set up. Servants of God we are, and we will not be in bondage to men.

As we are free from the conscription of the state, we must remember, also, that we are not eligible for its honors. I know you will say that is not a privilege, but it is a great benefit if looked at rightly. An Englishman in New York is not eligible for the very prickly throne of the president. I suppose he could not well be made a governor of Massachusetts or any other state, and, indeed, he may be well content to renounce the difficulties and the honor, too. So also, the Christian here is not eligible for this world's honors. It is a very bad sign to hear the world clap its hands, and say "Well done" to the Christian. He may begin to look to his standing and wonder whether he has not been doing wrong when the unrighteous give him their approval. "What, did I do wrong," said Socrates, "that yonder villain praised me just now?" And so may the Christian say, "What have I done wrong, that So-and-so spoke well of me, for if I had done right he would not. He has not the sense to praise goodness, he could only have applauded that which suited his own taste. Christians, we must never covet the world's esteem; the love of this world is not in keeping with the love of God. "If anyone loves the world, the love of the Father is not in him" (1 John 2:15). Treat its smiles as you treat its threats, with quiet contempt. Be willing rather to be sneered at than to be approved, counting the cross of Christ greater riches than all the treasures of Egypt. O harlot world, it were a sad dishonor to be your favorite. Adorn your head and paint your face, you Jezebel, but you are no friend of ours, nor will we desire your hollow love. The people of this world were insane to raise us to their seats of honor, for we are aliens and citizens of another country.

When the pope sent a noted Protestant statesman a present of some silver goblets, he returned them with this answer: "The citizens of Zurich compel their judges to swear twice in the year that they will receive no presents from foreign princes. Therefore take them back." More than twice in the year should the Christian resolve that he will not accept the smiles of this world and will do no homage to its glory. "We fear the Greeks even when they bear gifts." Like the Trojans of old, we may be beguiled with presents, even if we're not conquered by weapons. Renounce then the grandeur and honor of this fleeting age. Say in life what a proud cardinal said in death, "Vain pomp and glory of the world, I hate you." Pass through Vanity Fair without trading in its vanities, and cry in answer to their "What will you buy?", "We buy the truth." Take up the pilgrim's song and sing it always:

> The things eternal I pursue,
> And happiness beyond the view

Of those who basely pant
For things by nature felt and seen;

Their honors, wealth, and pleasures mean,
I neither have nor want.
Nothing on earth I call my own:
A stranger to the world unknown,

I all their goods despise;
I trample on their whole delight,
And seek a country out of sight,
A country in the skies.

Furthermore, as aliens, *it is not for us to hoard up this world's treasures.* Gentlemen, you who know the exchange of New York, would you hoard up any extensive amount of Mr. Chase's green backed notes? I think not. Those stamps which serve in the States in place of copper coinage, I should hardly desire to accumulate. Perhaps the fire might consume them, or if not, the gradual process of wear and tear which they are sure to undergo might leave me penniless before long. "No, sir," says the British trader, "I am an alien; I cannot very well accept payment in these bits of paper; they are very well for you. They will be accepted in your state, but my riches must be riches in England, for I am going there to live directly. I must have solid gold, old English sovereigns, nothing else but these can make me rich."

Brethren, so it is with us. If we are aliens, the treasures of this world are like those bits of paper, of little value in our esteem; and we should lay up our treasure in heaven, "where neither moth nor rust destroys and where thieves do not break in and steal" (Matthew 6:20). The money of this world

156

is not currency in Paradise, and when we reach its blissful shore, if regret were possible, we would wish we had laid up more treasure in the land of our fatherhood, in the dear fatherland beyond the skies. Transport your jewels to a safer country than this world. Be rich toward God rather than men.

A certain minister, collecting for a chapel, called on a rich merchant, who generously gave him fifty pounds. As the good man was going out with sparkling eye at the liberality of the merchant, the tradesman opened a letter and said, "Stop a minute. I find by this letter I have lost this morning a ship worth six thousand pounds." The poor minister trembled in his shoes, for he thought the next word would be, "Let me have the fifty-pound check back." Instead, he said, "Let me have the check back a moment." And then taking out his pen he wrote him a check for five hundred pounds. "As my money is going so fast, it is well," he said, "to make sure of some of it, so I will put some of it in God's bank." The man, you may be sure, went his way astonished at such a way of dealing. But indeed that is just what a man should do who feels he is an alien here and his treasure is beyond the sky.

> There is my house and portion fair;
> My treasure and my heart are there,
> And my abiding home:
> For me my elder brethren stay,
> And angels beckon me away,
> And Jesus bids me come.

Second, it is our comfort now to remind you that although we are aliens on earth, **we are citizens in heaven.**

What is meant by our being citizens in heaven? Why, first

that *we are under heaven's government.* Christ the king of heaven reigns in our hearts. The laws of glory are the laws of our consciences. Our daily prayer is, "Your will be done on earth as it is in heaven" (Matthew 6:10). The proclamations issued from the throne of glory are freely received by us; the decrees of the Great King we cheerfully obey. We are not without law to Christ. The Spirit of God rules in our mortal bodies; grace reigns through righteousness; and we wear the easy yoke of Jesus. O that He would sit as king in our hearts, like Solomon upon his throne of gold. Yours we are, Jesus, and all that we have. Rule us without a rival.

As citizens of the New Jerusalem, *we share heaven's honors.* The glory which belongs to glorified saints belongs to us, for we are already children of God, already subjects of the imperial line. Already we wear the spotless robe of Jesus' righteousness. Already we have angels for our servants, saints for our companions, Christ for our Brother, God for our Father, and a crown of immortality for our reward. We share the honors of citizenship, for we have come to the general assembly and Church of the firstborn, whose names are written in heaven. "Beloved, now we are children of God; and it has not yet been revealed what we shall be, but we know that when He is revealed, we shall be like Him, for we shall see Him as He is" (1 John 3:2).

As citizens, *we have common rights in all the property of heaven.* Those wide extensive plains we sang of just now are ours; ours the harps of gold and crowns of glory; ours the gates of pearl and walls of chrysolite; ours the azure light of the city that needs no candle nor light of the sun; ours the river of the water of life, and the twelve types of fruits which grow on the trees planted alongside the river. There is nothing in heaven that is not ours, for our citizenship is there. "Things present or things to come—all are yours. And you are Christ's, and Christ is God's" (1 Corinthians 3:22–23).

And as we are thus under heaven's government, and share its honors and partake of its possessions, so we today *enjoy its delights.* Do they rejoice over sinners that are born to God-prodigals who have returned? So do we. Do they chant the glories of triumphant grace? We do the same. Do they cast their crowns at Jesus' feet? Such honors as we have, we cast there too. Do they rejoice in Him? So also do we. Do they triumph, waiting for His second advent? By faith we triumph in the same. Are they tonight singing "Worthy the Lamb?" We also have sung the same tune, not to such glorious notes as theirs, but with as sincere hearts. With harmony not quite so splendid, but we hope as sincere, for the Spirit gave us the music that we have, and the Spirit gave them the thunders of their acclamations before the throne. "Our citizenship is in heaven."

Brethren, we rejoice to know also that as the result of our being citizens, or rather I ought to have said as the cause of it, our *names are written in the roll* of heaven's free citizens. When at last the list is read, our names will be read too; for where Paul and Peter, where David and Jonathan, where Abraham and Jacob will be found, we will be found too. Numbered with them we were in the divine purpose, reckoned with them we were in the purchase on the cross, and with them will we sit down forever at the tables of the blessed. The small and the great are fellow-citizens, and of the same household. The babes and the mature men are recorded in the same great registry, and neither death nor hell can erase a single name.

Our citizenship then is in heaven. We have not time to extend that thought. John Calvin says of this text, "It is a most abundant source of many exhortations, which it were easy for any one to elicit from it." We are not all Calvin; but even to our smaller capacities, the subject appears to be one not readily exhausted, but rich with unfathomable joy.

We must now come to our third point, which is, **our true life is in heaven,** our walk and acts are such as are consistent with our dignity *as citizens of heaven.* Among the old Romans, when an evil action was proposed it was thought a sufficient refusal to answer *"Romanus sum*—I am a Roman." Surely it should be a strong incentive to every good thing if we can claim to be citizens of the Eternal City. Let our lives be conformed to the glory of our citizenship. In heaven they are holy, so must we be—so are we if our citizenship is not a mere presence. They are happy, so must we be rejoicing in the Lord always. In heaven they are obedient; so must we be, following the faintest admonitions of the divine will. In heaven they are active; so should we be, both day and night praising and serving God. In heaven they are peaceful; so should we find a rest in Christ and be at peace even now. In heaven they rejoice to behold the face of Christ; so should we be always meditating upon Him, studying His beauties, and desiring to look into the truths He has taught. In heaven they are full of love; so should we love one another as brethren. In heaven they have sweet communion one with another; so should we, who though many, are one body, be every one members one of the other.

Before the throne they are free from envy and strife, ill-will, jealousy, contention, falsehood, anger; and so should we be. We should, in fact, seek while we are here to keep up the manners and customs of the good old fatherland, so that, as in Paris the Parisian soon says, "There goes John Bull," so they should be able to say in this land, "There goes a heavenly citizen, one who is with us, and among us, but is not of us." Our very speech should be such that our citizenship should be detected. We should not be able to live long in a house without men finding out what we are.

A friend of mine once went across to America, and landing, I think, at Boston, he knew nobody. But hearing a man say, when somebody had dropped a small barrel on the loading dock, "Look out there, or else you will make a Coggeshall job of it," he said, "You are an Essex man, I know, for that is a proverb never used anywhere but in Essex; give me your hand." And they were friends at once. So there should be a ring of true metal about our speech and behavior, so that when a brother meets us, he can say, "You are a Christian, I know, for none but Christians speak like that, or act like that." "Surely you also are one of them, for your speech betrays you" (Matthew 26:73).

Our holiness should act as a sort of fraternity by which we know how to give the grip to the stranger, who is not a real stranger but a fellow citizen with us, and of the household of faith. O, dear friends, wherever we wander, we should never forget our beloved land. In Australia, on the other side the world, or in the Cape of Good Hope, or wherever else we may be exiled, surely every Englishman's eye must turn to this fair island. And with all her faults, we must love her still. And surely let us be where we may, but our eyes must turn to heaven, the happy land unstained by shadow of fault. We love her still and love her more and more, praying for the time when our exile will expire and we will enter into our fatherland to dwell there forever and ever. Shenstone says, "The proper means of increasing the love we bear our native country is to reside some time in a foreign land." I am certain that we who cry, "Woe is me, that I dwell in Meshech, that I dwell among the tents of Kedar!" (Psalm 120:5), are sure to add, "Oh, that I had wings like a dove! I would fly away and be at rest" (Psalm 55:6).

The text says, "Our citizenship is in heaven," and I think we may read it as though it said, fourth, **our commerce is in heaven.** We are trading on earth, but still the bulk of our trade is with heaven. We trade for trinkets in this land, but our gold and silver are in heaven.

We commune with heaven, and how? Our trade is with heaven by *meditation*—we often think of God our Father and Christ our Brother. And, by the Spirit, the Comforter, we are brought in contemplative delight to the general assembly and Church of the firstborn, whose names are written in heaven. Brethren, do not our *thoughts* sometimes burn within us when we trade with that blessed land? When I have sent the ships of understanding and consideration to that land of Ophir, which is full of gold, and they have come back again laden with all manner of precious things, my thoughts have been enriched, my soul has longed to journey to that good land. Black and stormy you are, O sea of death, but I would cross you to reach that land of Havilah, which has dust of gold. I know that he who is a Christian will never have his mind long off that better land. And do you know we sometimes trade with heaven in our hymns? They tell us of the Swiss troops in foreign countries, that there is a song which the band is forbidden to play because it reminds them of the cowbells of their native hills. If the men hear it, they are sure to desert, for that dear old song revives before their eyes the wooden chalets and the cows and the pastures of the glorious Alps, and they long to be away. There are some of our hymns that make us homesick, until we are hardly content to stop. And therefore, well did our poet end his song,

> Filled with delight, my raptured soul,
> Can here no longer stay.
> Though Jordan's waves around us roll,
> Fearless we launch away.

I feel the spirit of Wesley when he said,

> O that we now might see our guide!
> O that the word were given!
> Come, Lord of hosts, the waves divide,
> And land us all in heaven.

In times of high, hallowed, heavenly harmony of praise, the songs of angels seem to come astray and find their way down to us. And then our songs return with them, hand in hand, and go back to God's throne, through Jesus Christ.

We trade with heaven, I hope, too, not only thus by meditation, and by thought, and by song, but *by hopes and by loves*. Our love is toward that land. How heartily the Germans sing of the dear old fatherland. But they cannot, with all their Germanic patriotism, beat the genial glow of the Briton's heart, when he thinks of his fatherland too. The Scotchman, too, wherever he may be, remembers the land of "brown heath and shaggy wood." And the Irishman, too, let him be where he will, still thinks the "Emerald Isle" the first gem of the sea. It is right that the patriot should love his country. Does not our love fervently flame towards heaven?

We think we cannot speak well enough of it, and indeed here we are correct, for no exaggeration is possible. When we talk of that land of Eshcol, our mouths are watering to taste its clusters; already, like David, we thirst to drink of the well that is within the gate; and we hunger after the good grain of the land.

Our ears want to be done with the discords of earth so that they may open to the harmonies of heaven. And our tongues are longing to sing the melodious sonnets, sung by flaming ones above. Yes, we do love heaven, and thus it is that we prove that our commerce is with that better land.

Brethren, just as people in a foreign land who love their country always are glad to have plenty of letters from the country, I hope we have much *communication with the old fatherland.* We send our prayers there as letters to our Father, and we get His letters back in this blessed volume of His Word. You go into an Australian settler's hut, and you find a newspaper. Where from, sir? A gazette from the south of France, a journal from America? Oh no, it is a newspaper from England, addressed to him in his old mother's hand-writing, bearing the postage stamp with the good Queen's face in the corner. And he likes it, though it be only a news-paper from some little insignificant country town, with no news in it. Yet he likes it better, perhaps, than the *Times* itself, because it talks to him about the village where he lived and consequently touches a special string in the harp of his soul. So must it be with heaven. This book, the Bible, is the news-paper of heaven, and therefore we must love it. The sermons which are preached are good news from a far country. The hymns we sing are notes by which we tell our Father of our welfare here and by which He whispers into our soul His continued love to us. All these are and must be pleasant to us, for our commerce is with heaven.

I hope, too, we are sending a good deal home. I like to see our young fellows, when they go out to live in the bush, recollect their mother at home. They say, "She had a hard struggle to bring us up when our father died, and she scraped her little together to help us to emigrate." John and Tom mutually agree, "The first gold we get at the diggings we will send home to mother." And it goes home. Well, I hope you are sending a great many things home. Dear friends, I hope as we are aliens here, we are not laying up our treasure here, where we may lose it, but packing it off as quickly as we can to our own country. There are many ways of doing it. God has many banks, and they are all safe ones. We have but to serve His Church, or serve the souls which Christ has bought with His blood, or help His poor, clothe His naked, and feed His hungry, and we send our treasures beyond the sea in a safe ship. And so we keep up our commerce with the skies.

Time has gone; those clocks will strike when thy ought not. There is a great reason why we should live like aliens and foreigners here, and that is, fifth, **Christ is coming soon.** The early Church never forgot this. Did they not pant and thirst after the return of their ascended Lord? Like the twelve tribes, day and night they instantly watched for Messiah. But the Church has grown weary of this hope. There have been so many false prophets who tell us that Christ is coming, that the Church thinks He never will come. And she begins to deny, or to keep in the background, the blessed doctrine of the second advent of her Lord from heaven. I do not think the fact that there have been many false prophets should make us doubt our Lord's true word. Perhaps the very frequency of these mistakes may show that there is truth at the bottom. You have a friend who is ill, and the doctor says he cannot last long; he must die. You have called a great many times expecting to hear of his departure, but he is still alive. Now the frequent errors of the physicians do not prove that your friend will not die one of these days, and that speedily too. And so, though the false prophets have said, "Lo, here," and "Lo, there," and yet Christ has not come, that does not prove that His glorious appearing will never arrive.

You know I am no prophet. I do not know anything about 1866; I find quite enough to do to attend to 1862. I do not understand the visions of Daniel or Ezekiel; I find I have enough to do to teach the simple word such as I find in Matthew, Mark, Luke, and John, and the Epistles of Paul. I do not find many souls have been converted to God by exquisite dissertations about the battle of Armageddon, and all those other fine things. I have no doubt prophesyings are very profitable, but I rather question whether they are so profitable to the hearers as they may be to the preachers and publishers. I conceive that among religious people of a certain sort, the abortive explanations of prophecy issued by certain doctors gratify a craving, which in irreligious people finds its food in novels and romances.

People have a panting to know the future. And certain divines pander to this depraved taste by prophesying for them and letting them know what is coming by-and-by. I do not know the future, and I will not pretend to know. But I do preach this because I know it, that *Christ will come,* for he says so in a hundred passages. The Epistles of Paul are full of the advent, and Peter's too, and John's letters are crowded with it. The best of saints have always lived on the hope of the advent. There was Enoch; he prophesied of the coming of the Son of Man. So there was another Enoch who was always talking of the coming, and saying, "Come quickly." I will not divide the house tonight by discussing whether the advent will be premillennial or postmillennial, or anything of that. It is enough for me that *He will come,* and "the Son of Man is coming at an hour you do not expect" (Matt. 24:44). Tonight He may appear, while we stand here; just when we think that He will not come, the thief will break open the house. We ought, therefore, to be always watching. Since the gold and silver that you have will be worthless at His advent; since your lands and estates will melt to smoke when He appears; since *then* the righteous will be rich and the godly will be great, do not lay up your treasure here, for it may at any time vanish, at any time disappear, for Christ may at any moment come.

I think the Church would do well to be always living as if Christ might come today. I feel persuaded she is doing ill if she works as if He would not come until 1866 because He may come before and He may come this moment. Let her always be living as if He would come *now,* still acting in her Master's sight and watching unto prayer. Never mind about the last bowls fill your own bowl with sweet odors and offer it before the Lord. Think what you like about Armageddon, but do not forget to fight the good fight of faith. Guess not at the precise era for the destruction of Antichrist; go and destroy it yourself, fighting against it every day. But be looking forward and hastening unto the coming of the Son of Man, and let this be at once your comfort and excitement to diligence, that the Savior will soon come from heaven.

Now, I think you foreigners here present—and I hope

there are a great many true aliens here—ought to feel like a poor stranded mariner on a desolate island who has saved a few things from the wreck, built himself an old log hut, and has a few comforts round about him; but for all that, he longs for home. Every morning he looks out to sea and wonders when he will see a sail. Many times while examining the wide ocean to look for a ship, he has clapped his hands and then wept to find he was disappointed. Every night he lights his fire that there may be a blaze, so that if a ship should go by, they may send relief to the stranded mariner. Ah! That is just the way we ought to live. We have heard of one saint who used to open his window every morning when he woke, to see if Christ had come. It might be fanaticism, but better to be enthusiastic than to mind earthly things. I would have us look out each night and light the fire of prayer, that it may be burning in case the ships of heaven should go by, that blessings may come to us poor aliens and foreigners who need them so much. Let us wait patiently until the Lord's convoy takes us on board, that we may be carried into the glories and splendor of the reign of Christ. Let us always hold the log hut with a loose hand and long for the time when we will get to that better land where our possessions are, where our Father lives, where our treasures lie, where all our brethren dwell. Well said our poet —

> Blest scenes,
> through rude and stormy seas
> I onward press to you.

My beloved friends, I can assure you it is always one of the sweetest thoughts I ever know, that I will meet with you in heaven. There are so many of you members of this Church that I can hardly get to shake hands with you once in a year, but I will have plenty of time then in heaven. You will know your pastor in heaven better than you do now. He loves you now, and you love him. We will then have more time to recount our experience of divine grace, and praise God together, and sing together, and rejoice together concerning Him by whom we were helped to plant, and sow, and through whom all the increase came.

> I hope when days and years are past,
> We all shall meet in heaven,
> We all shall meet in heaven at last,
> We all shall meet in heaven.

But we will not all meet in glory not all—unless you repent. Some of you will certainly perish unless you believe in Christ. But why must we be divided? O why not all in heaven? "Believe on the Lord Jesus Christ, and you will be saved" (Acts 16:31). "He who believes and is baptized will be saved; but he who does not believe will be condemned" (Mark 16:16). Trust Christ, sinner, and heaven is yours, and mine, and we are safe forever. Amen.

Study Guide

———=◉=———

Why Government Can't Save You

CHAPTER 1
POLITICAL INVOLVEMENT:
A CHRISTIAN PERSPECTIVE

Getting Started

1. What specific departure from biblical standards and morality concerns you most today? Why? Have you had any firsthand encounter with this particular problem? If so, how did you deal with it?

2. What is the most important lesson you have learned from your own past mistakes? How did that lesson change your life?

Answering the Questions

1. Compare the social values of an average '50s teen to those of an average teen today.

2. List five practices in contemporary culture that you think ought to alarm believers.

3. How has democracy and political freedom been linked to Christianity during the past two centuries? Does such a connection justify the American Revolution?

4. How does the Prohibition Movement of the late 1800s parallel many of the tactics of recent Christian prolife activists?

5. What degree of involvement in politics and social causes should believers have? How does complete noninvolvement violate God's Word, and what wrong attitudes does it reveal?

6. How do examples of Joseph, Daniel, and Cornelius, who worked as public servants, show us that God does not prohibit our involvement in government?

7. What is the core issue concerning the amount of our involvement in government and politics? How should this affect our service to God (see Exodus 19:6; 1 Peter 2:9)?

8. What political and social factors during Jesus' time made life so difficult for the Jews?

9. How should Jesus' command for us to carry on His ministry priorities (Matthew 28:18–20) mesh with out political and social activities?

10. What short, well-known passage summarizes Jesus' command for us to carry on His ministry priorities?

Focusing on Prayer

- Ask the Lord to grant you the desire to have a balanced, Christlike perspective on the church's involvement in politics and the understanding to apply it wisely.
- Pray that God will remove any antagonism you might have toward the many unbelievers who are enslaved to the destructive, harmful practices and ideas of today's culture. Ask that you are able to show mercy to them as He's shown mercy to you. Then ask God to free them from their sins and turn their hearts to Him.

Applying the Truth

Reread the quote from Robert L. Ottley concerning the Old Testament prophets. Then over the next week or two read one of the major prophets, such as Isaiah or Jeremiah, and note the places where you see Ottley's analysis verified. What did you learn about the prophet's heart for the world and people? How can you apply that to your ministry to others?

CHAPTER 2
OUR RESPONSIBILITY TO AUTHORITY

Getting Started

1. Do you think it's okay for a Christian to belong to a labor or professional union, especially if that group might some day vote to strike? What would it mean to you if membership is required to hold a particular position (teacher, firefighter, police officer, civil servant)?

2. It's not always easy to accept the laws and directives issued by ungodly authority. Describe a struggle you've had with such compliance. How did you eventually resolve the tension?

Answering the Questions

1. What is the essence of Paul's statement in Romans 13:1? Are there any limitations to our subjection?
2. What principle did the two Jewish midwives in Exodus 1 exemplify?
3. What is especially commendable about the manner in which Daniel and his three friends differed with the king's dietary request (Daniel 1:8, 12–14)?
4. How often will most of us have to follow the apostles' example and "obey God rather than men"? What situation would require civil disobedience from you?
5. How in the past decade have professed believers gone to excess in protesting evil in society?
6. What truth does David reveal in Psalm 62:11?
7. What significant role concerning world and national affairs has God permitted for Satan?
8. What is rebellion against the government equivalent to? How seriously does God view this (Numbers 16)?
9. To be biblically based and effective, punishment must: (1) fit the offense, (2) be viewed as a deterrent to crime, (3) be administered impartially, (4) be applied without delay, and (5) be balanced with mercy. Which of these are missing from our legal system?
10. In its responsibility toward government, how did the ancient church compare to ours today?

Focusing on Prayer
- Confess any ways in which you have failed in your scriptural responsibility toward authority. Ask the Lord to give you a better understanding of the principle of civil obedience and the reasons to obey it.
- Pray that your local church, in all it does and says, will be a godly society within your larger, ungodly community.

Applying the Truth

Read Psalm 62:11 and Jeremiah 29:7. Choose one to memorize this week.

CHAPTER 3
THE BIBLICAL PURPOSE OF GOVERNMENT

Getting Started

1. Have you ever been a member of a club, professional society, association of hobby enthusiasts, or any other organized group that seemed to stray from its original purpose? How frustrating was that for you? Did you try to persuade the leaders or other members to get back to the original objectives? Discuss your experience.
2. In what ways do you think our government fails most in meeting its biblical purposes—to restrain evil, to protect and support us, or to punish lawbreakers? Why?

Answering the Questions

1. What role do you think terror from authorities should play in controlling flagrant lawbreakers? How can the form of government determine how effective this terror is?

2. If you were the governor of your state, what new program would you develop to reduce crime?

3. How has the knowledge of good and evil, passed on to every human being since Adam and Eve, affected us all—even unbelievers? Does that mean everyone is born with a conscience?

4. Why is basic morality crucial to a viable social order and cultural stability?

5. What is your definition of a good citizen? How does government generally treat such a person?

6. What specifically in Romans 13:4 indicates that *all* rulers at *all* levels deserve our honor and respect?

7. How early in mankind's existence did God institute capital punishment (Genesis 9:6)? How do you feel the government should administer this punishment?

8. How do you think God views nations that outlaw capital punishment or seldom carry it out (see Ezra 7:26)?

9. How well have prisons worked in modern America? What do you think would happen to our crime statistics if we did like the Jews and promptly executed criminals or required restitution rather than imprisonment?

10. What does Paul mention as a loftier motivation for believers in maintaining good citizenship (Romans 13:5)? Why does that motivation work?

Focusing on Prayer

- Find out who your leaders are at all levels of government. Pray for them by name and ask that they be diligent and sense their divinely ordained mandate as they seek to restrain evil and promote good in the community.
- If you know someone who is now imprisoned or of a family who has a member in prison, pray that the Holy Spirit would both convict and encourage that person as he or she serves time. Ask God for that person to be able to repay his victims and regain a sense of dignity through genuine salvation.

Applying the Truth

Write a brief letter of support to one of your local government or law enforcement officials. Without getting "preachy" tell them you are praying for them—then do it.

CHAPTER 4
OUR TAX OBLIGATION

Getting Started

1. Among the various taxes you have to pay, do you feel any are unfair or levied at too high a percentage rate? Which ones are they, and why do you feel that way? How do you maintain a proper attitude toward such taxes?
2. Our leaders often seem to use tax revenue unwisely

or for the wrong things. If you had the authority, how would you reallocate some tax money? Explain your reasons.

Answering the Questions

1. Look back in the chapter and review how the government in Rome displayed its ungodliness and inequities. In what ways do you see evidence of that behavior in our government?
2. Why were national tax collectors so hated throughout the Roman Empire?
3. Read Romans 13:1–8. What is Paul's view of tax payments? Why was Paul so adamant about it?
4. Scripture first mentions a form of national taxes in Genesis 41:33–36. What would have been the result had Pharaoh not listened to Joseph's advice?
5. Reread the section called "Jewish Tax System." What was the total annual rate of the six taxes and tithes the Lord mandated under the Law for the nation of Israel? How does that compare to your tax rate?
6. According to Matthew 22:15–22, what did Jesus teach concerning taxes? Why do you think His response here was politically wise?
7. What is the significance of the Greek word for "ministers" in Romans 13:6? Who is it defining in this context?
8. How does the apostle Paul's command in Romans 13:7 reinforce Jesus' teaching in Matthew 22:21?
9. How would the quality of life change in your city if everyone paid what they felt to be fair taxes?

10.   Read Deuteronomy 12:10–19. As a citizen, what lesson on national unity and cooperation can you draw from the passage?

Focusing on Prayer

• Spend some time this week asking God to examine your heart attitude toward paying taxes. Confess any sin He reveals, and ask Him to help you turn from it and adopt a godly attitude toward *all* aspects of your tax obligation.

• Pray that your leaders would have wisdom and discernment in fairly administering tax requirements and prudently spending the revenue.

Applying the Truth

Make a list of all the good things you can think of that are paid for by your taxes. Spend time thanking God for each one.

CHAPTER 5
JESUS' LESSON ON TAX EXEMPTIONS

Getting Started

1.   Have you ever been concerned about being able to pay your taxes? Share with the group the most interesting or creative way you found the money to pay your tax bill. Or, share briefly a unique way you spent a tax refund check.

2. What style of supervision do you prefer from your boss in the workplace—a hands-on, involved style, or the more hands-off style that lets the employee be a self-starter? Why? If you're a manager, explain why you use one style or the other.

Answering the Questions

1. What was the greatest hands-on lesson you ever learned about paying taxes? Who taught it to you?

2. What was interesting and perhaps a bit ironic about the timing of Jesus' tax instruction to Peter (Matthew 17:24–27)?

3. Where did the confrontation over taxes take place, and why do you think it involved just Jesus and Peter?

4. In Bible times the temple tax was collected so that the Jews would have funds to operate the Jerusalem temple. How would you react to such a tax today?

5. Why do you think Peter was curious about Jesus' position on paying taxes?

6. As the son of God, Jesus could have claimed exemption from the temple tax. Why didn't He? How do you know when claiming tax exemptions is wrong?

7. What type of coin did Peter find in the fish's mouth? Why was it particularly useful for his needs? (See Matthew 17:24–27).

8. Has God ever provided tax money for you just when you needed it? If so, in what way?

9. How in the New Testament has the Holy Spirit turned the harsh and dreary terminology of slavery into something positive?

10. What responsibilities should our heavenly citizenship remind us of (see 1 Peter 2:11–12)?

Focusing on Prayer

- Ask the Lord to help you trust Him more during the coming year to provide the resources you need to pay your various taxes. Thank Him in advance for His faithful provision.
- Thank God this week for the privilege of being a heavenly citizen. Pray also that you would live worthy of being part of his family.

Applying the Truth

Read 1 Peter 2:9; 2:11–12. Spend time praising God in song for choosing you to be His child. Praise Him for the abundance of all your heavenly riches.

CHAPTER 6
SUPPORTING OUR LEADERS: HOW AND WHY

Getting Started (Choose One)

1. Think about a time when you did something unwise or even reckless and someone held you accountable for it. How did you respond to their reprimand? What approach would have gotten the best response from you?
2. Has it ever been challenging for you to support a new boss? How did you overcome your negative feelings. What did you learn from that experience?

Answering the Questions

1. Which early Christians do you consider good examples of citizens who boldly supported their government despite their personal treatment? What was so remarkable about their statements?

2. In the early decades of Christianity, how did most Roman officials view Christians? What shameful behaviors did they wrongly charge believers with?

3. What false accusations have you heard leveled against believers in today's media? What do you think our reaction to them should be?

4. With what has the world always associated the attitude of submission?

5. After God judged Nebuchadnezzar for his arrogance (Daniel 4:30–34), what was that king constrained to acknowledge (see Psalms 92:8; 93:1–2)?

6. What effects are inevitable when government leadership becomes too detached from God's principles? What reminder from believers would help prevent or delay those?

7. Look back in the chapters under "Leaders Have Civic Duties." What four specific responsibilities should we remind our leaders of as part of their general faithfulness to civic duties?

8. What is the wisest way we as Christians can offer reminders and lend support to our leaders?

9. What responsible limit does God place on our life of liberty in Christ (see 1 Peter 2:16)?

10. What benefits result from our support of authority?

Focusing on Prayer

- Ask the Lord to help you better follow the pattern of early church leaders such as Clement of Rome, Justin Martyr, and Tertullian as you support your government leaders.
- Spend extra time praising and thanking God that He is sovereign over world affairs and in His appointment of rulers. Pray for the leaders of other countries by name.

Applying the Truth

Obtain the names and addresses of all your government officials—local, state, and national. List these in a notebook or daily planner, and begin praying regularly for each person. Occasionally send them written notes or e-mail messages reminding them of their accountability as leaders and telling them of your prayers for them. Be sure to record answers to specific requests.

CHAPTER 7
DANIEL'S UNCOMPROMISING CIVIL SERVICE

Getting Started (Choose One)

1. Experts have always extolled the virtues of good educational preparation. But what kind is best—four or more years of college, or several years of high-tech training in a very specific area of application? How has your own training helped or hindered you in obtaining jobs? Discuss.

2. Would you encourage a young person in your church to pursue a career in politics or government service? Why or why not?

Answering the Questions

1. Ezekiel, one of Daniel's contemporaries, recognized his greatness as a role model. Who is your contemporary whom you consider a Daniel? How are they alike?
2. What do you see as challenging for Daniel during his rise to prominence?
3. What factors helped influence the choice of Daniel and his companions for royal service under Nebuchadnezzar (Daniel 1:4)?
4. What were the positive and negative aspects of Daniel's reeducation process? Why did he have to exercise great discernment?
5. What's the likeliest reason that the Babylonian officials urged Daniel and his friends to partake of the royal food and drink? Why did Daniel take such a strong position against indulging?
6. When have you seen Christians take a strong, godly position in a self-righteous, ungodly way? How did others react to their behavior? How did it affect their witness for Christ?
7. How did Daniel apply Proverbs 29:25 in making the dietary issues clear to his superiors?
8. What did Daniel's willingness to submit to a ten-day test involving no meat or wine reveal about his character?

9. How has God blessed you personally when you have chosen to live uncompromisingly?

10. What does Daniel's success in government tell you about God's involvement in politics?

Focusing on Prayer

- Pray that God would grant you the wisdom and courage not to be intimidated or perplexed when your convictions are tested.

- Pray that your city and county officials (police, judges, etc.) administer justice honestly and fairly. Pray for as many as you can by name.

Applying the Truth

Reread Daniel 1:8–15. Test yourself by eating Daniel's diet for ten days. During that time, pray for wisdom and for courage to stand for your conviction in a godly way.

CHAPTER 8
PAUL'S EXAMPLE BEFORE WORLDLY AUTHORITIES

Getting Started (Choose One)

1. Voter turnout in American elections is now much lower than it was several generations ago. In your opinion, what is the main reason for this phenomenon? Do you find it a pleasure or a hassle to exercise your right to vote? Why?

2. Which category do you think is more difficult to deal with and submit to in a dispute: unsympathetic religious leaders, or indifferent and apathetic secular authorities? Explain your answer and, if possible, relate a specific experience you've had that proves your point.

Answering the Questions

1. How might Paul's rights as a Roman citizen have affected the way he conducted himself when he was arrested? When have you felt your rights were violated (as a citizen, as a spouse, as an employee, etc.)? How did you react?

2. What two major religious factions dominated the Sanhedrin (Acts 23:6)?

3. Why was Paul's confidence so high as he addressed the Sanhedrin in Acts 23:1?

4. The conscience is not always a reliable guide for our words and actions, otherwise Saul's would not have allowed him to persecute Christians. With Saul, what was lacking? (see 1 Corinthians 2:14–15; 4:4.)

5. What sparked Paul's anger at his hearing (Acts 23:1–3)? Was it justified? When have you had to restrain your actions and submit even though you were right? When have you reacted angrily, willing to suffer the consequences? What determines your decision to react boldly?

6. What did Paul's angry reaction toward the high priest reveal was still true about the apostle (Romans 7:14–25)? How was the way he handled the reprimand for his outburst wise and what did that response show concerning his character (Acts 23:5)?

7. How were Paul's beliefs on certain doctrinal matters more compatible with the Pharisees than the Sadducees (Acts 23:6–9)?

8. Because of Paul's drastic, sudden change from zealous Pharisee to zealous Christian, neither side trusted him. When have you experienced such a situation in your church?

9. The Jews were repeatedly unable to make their charges against Paul stick. What does that fact underscore about the character of Paul and other early Christians?

10. The chapter section "Lessons from Paul" Names four lessons we can glean from the apostle's experiences before worldly authorities. What other lessons did Paul teach you?

Focusing on Prayer

- Thank God for Paul's righteous example in relating to authority. Pray that you would live in a way that reflects that legacy.
- Pray for the leaders of nations where Christians are persecuted. Ask that the hearts of those leaders be changed for good.

Applying the Truth

Watch the news or ask your missions ministry for the names of countries where Christians are being persecuted. Try to get specific names of Christians so you can send or e-mail them encouragement and support.

CHAPTER 9
HOW TO LIVE IN A PAGAN CULTURE

Getting Started

1. What sorts of things can happen when people forget or stray from their life's priorities or calling? How have you experienced that?
2. Do you think people are more prone, less prone, or equally prone to criticize worldly institutions when they're first saved than they are after being Christians for a while? Explain your answer, based on your observations and experiences.

Answering the Questions

1. What attitude can we take that will ensure that unbelievers will ignore or reject our message? What one Christian trait can by itself make the lost more receptive to the gospel?
2. Why is it so harmful and wrong "to speak evil" of someone? What especially does it reveal about us when we direct it at rulers and leaders?
3. Which one of our duties listed in Titus 3:2 is also a beatitude and an aspect of the fruit of the Holy Spirit?
4. What moral and spiritual situation has characterized the world since the Fall? What should Titus 3:1–8 keep us mindful of and motivate us to do?
5. Why is "humility to all men" important in our Christian walk in a pagan society?

6. What all is involved in being born again (see Titus 3:1–8)?

7. As a result of God's love and kindness, what can you reflect on and be grateful for in your life?

8. Salvation has delivered us from spiritual death, but what spiritual privileges do we receive? (See John 3:16; Ephesians 2:5; Colossians 1:13; 1 Timothy 2:4; Titus 1:2).

9. What is necessary for regeneration (see John 3:5, 7; Ephesians 5:26)?

10. What does 2 Corinthians 5:17 say about the beginning of the Holy Spirit's sanctifying work in our lives?

Focusing on Prayer
- Ask the Lord to give you a greater sense of daily gratitude as you reflect on your past unsaved condition and your present condition of salvation.
- Pray that the genuine message of salvation would prevail over all other messages that futilely seek to reform society along external moral and political lines. Ask God to grant you and other believers a renewed dedication to our primary mission.

Applying the Truth

Reread the list of Christian duties in Titus 3:1–2. Select one or two that you need to improve in, and then do some additional Bible study on the key words and concepts involved. Pray that God would show you a tangible way to minister one of these actions in the life of those around you.

Endnotes

CHAPTER ONE

1. *Aspects of the Old Testament.* The Bampton Lectures, 1897 (London: Longmans, 1898), 430–31.
2. *The Evangelical Pulpit* (Grand Rapids: Baker, 1993), 106–7.

CHAPTER 2

1. *An Exposition of Romans* (McLean, Va.: MacDonald Publishing, n.d.), 579.
2. *Apology, XXX, XXXI, XXXII; The Ante-Nicene Fathers* (reprint; Grand Rapids: Eerdmans, 1973), 3:42–43.

CHAPTER 3

1. Richard D. Heffner, *A Documentary History of the United States* (New York: New American Library/ Mentor Books, 1956, 1965), 51–52.
2. *An Exposition of Romans* (McLean, Va.: MacDonald Publishing, n.d.), 581.
3. *Toward a Biblical View of Civil Government* (Chicago: Moody Press, 1974), 256.

CHAPTER 6

1. 1 Clement lx.2-lxi.2. Cited in F.F. Bruce, *The Epistle of Paul to the Romans* (London: Tyndale Press, 1967), 235.
2. "First Apology of Justin," chapter 27 in *The Ante-Nicene Fathers,* vol. 1, Alexander Roberts and James Donaldson, ed. (Grand Rapids: Eerdmans, 1973 reprint), 168.
3. "Apology," chapter 30 in *The Ante-Nicene Fathers,* 3:42.
4. cited by William Barclay in *The Letters of James and Peter,* rev. ed. (Philadelphia: Westminster, 1976), 202.
5. *Toward a Biblical View of Civil Government* (Chicago: Moody Press, 1974), 78–79.
6. *Toward a Biblical View of Civil Government* (Chicago: Moody Press, 1974), 256.

CHAPTER 8

1. *Paul the Apostle* (Chicago: Moody Press, 1986), 13.

Also from John MacArthur

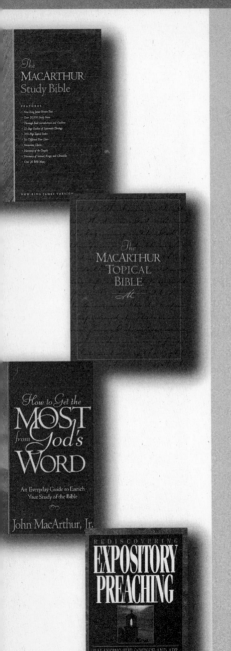

The MacArthur Study Bible
Featuring the word-for-word accuracy
of the New King James Version, *The
MacArthur Study Bible* is perfect for serious
study. Pastor/teacher John MacArthur has
compiled more than 20,000 study notes,
a 200-page topical index, and numerous
charts, maps, outlines, and articles.
Winner of "The 1998 Study Bible of
the Year Award."

The MacArthur Topical Bible
An invaluable tool for tracing topics
throughout the Bible. For each word or
topic in the Bible, a definition and
explanation is given, beginning with Aaron
and ending with Zebulun. Subtopics are
listed and beneath each subtopic, verses
are quoted with references in order of
the books of the Bible. A must-have
for all Bible students.

How to Get the Most from God's Word
From one of today's most popular Bible
speakers, you can learn to effectively apply
Bible teachings and principles to your own
life. This practical Bible study companion
cuts to the heart of God's Word and shows
you how to do the same.

Rediscovering Expository Preaching
John MacArthur and his colleagues at The
Master's Seminary offer a definitive manual
on "rightly dividing the Word of truth" for
today's congregations. With insight and
clarity, they examine the four steps of Bible
exposition, emphasizing the role of study
and prayer in sermon preparation.

The Murder of Jesus
Two thousand years ago, an unprecedented conspiracy of injustice, cruelty, religious and political interests sentenced a man guilty of no crimes to the most barbaric method of execution ever devised. Piecing together the narrative from the perspective of the participants, MacArthur relives the most awesome injustice in the history of man and the unparalleled triumph of the sovereignty of God.

The Gospel According to the Apostles
John MacArthur takes a solid look at some of the most divisive faith issues in evangelical circles today. Presenting a thorough discussion of the "lordship salvation," he addresses such issues as assurance of salvation, righteousness and imperfection, "cheap grace," and the importance of obedience in the Christian life.

The Vanishing Conscience
In this compelling book, MacArthur sounds a wake-up call for Christians to confront society's flight from moral responsibility and recognize sin for what it is. In doing so, he says, we can move from living a life of blame and denial to one of true peace and freedom.

Introduction to Biblical Counseling
Solid theological foundations of biblical counseling are clearly presented in contrast to humanistic and secular theories of psychological counseling. A practical, proactive, and relevant book for students, church leaders, and lay people. This collection of writers represents some of America's leading biblical teachers and counselors.

Rediscovering Pastoral Ministry
Encouraging, insightful and challenging, Rediscovering Pastoral Ministry is designed for a new generation of shepherds who seek to lead with the passion of the apostles. Written by MacArthur and his colleagues at The Master's Seminary, this guide outlines the biblical priorities essential to effective ministry.

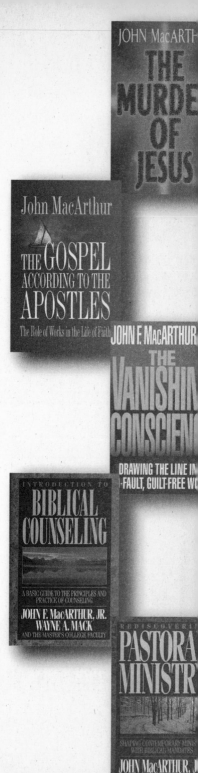

The Bible for Life series

What the Bible Says About Parenting
More than ever, Christians need to know what the Bible teaches about parenting. Pastor/teacher John MacArthur presents time proven principles of biblical parenting clearly and carefully to help parents make sense of their duties before God and to bring up their children in the ways of the Lord.

Whose Money Is It, Anyway?
In this no-nonsense, practical book, renowned Bible scholar John MacArthur cuts through popular opinion to the core of what the Bible says about money and materialism. Discussing the topics of instant gratification, giving, and success, MacArthur challenges readers to loosen their grip on their purse strings and instead turn their focus towards a richer relationship with God.

Why Government Can't Save You
Renowned pastor and author John MacArthur delves into what the Bible says about a Christian's responsibility toward authority, the biblical purposes of government, and how to support our governmental leaders. Using Paul's example before worldly authorities and Jesus' lessons to Peter, MacArthur challenges Christians to remember our true status as we act responsibly in matters of politics.

How to Survive in a World of Unbelievers
On the night of His betrayal, Jesus delivered some of the most poignant, powerful teaching in all of his ministry on earth. It was a momentous transition—the New Testament age was beginning. In this book, pastor/teacher John MacArthur examines the powerful legacy Jesus laid out for his disciples at the Last Supper—the legacy that is ours to claim as His followers.

The MacArthur Bible Studies

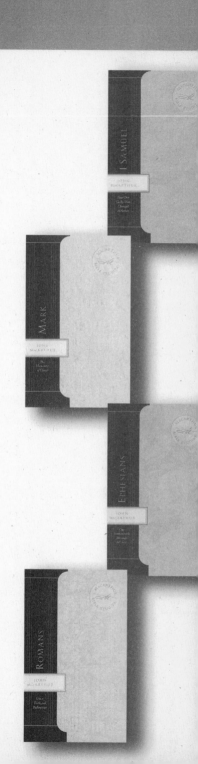

I Samuel

Learn from Bible expositor John MacArthur about Samuel, a man of God, who shows us how one godly person can influence a whole nation for positive change—a message we desperately need to hear today in our world. The MacArthur Bible Study series is excellent for personal devotions, small group study, adult Bible classes, and other Bible study opportunities.

Mark

Learn from Bible expositor John MacArthur about the joys and trials of God's only Son, which can lead us to a better understanding of how great His saving love is. The MacArthur Bible Study series is excellent for personal devotions, small group study, adult Bible classes, and other Bible study opportunities.

Romans

Learn from Bible expositor John MacArthur about the righteousness that comes from God and the truth that God justifies guilty, condemned sinners by grace through faith in Christ alone. The MacArthur Bible Study series is excellent for personal devotions, small group study, adult Bible classes, and other Bible study opportunities.

Ephesians

Learn from Bible expositor John MacArthur as he unravels the glories and mysteries of the church of Jesus, helping us to better understand the immeasurable blessings God has for us. The MacArthur Bible Study series is excellent for personal devotions, small group study, adult Bible classes, and other Bible study opportunities.